It's Only a Flat Tire in the Rain

It's Only a Flat Tire in the Rain

Navigating Life's Bumpy Roads
with Faith and Grace

Max Davis, M.A.

A PERIGEE BOOK

A Perigee Book
Published by The Berkley Publishing Group
A division of Penguin Putnam Inc.
375 Hudson Street
New York, New York 10014

G. P. Putnam's Sons edition: January 2001
First Perigee edition: January 2002

Perigee ISBN: 0-399-52740-0

Visit our website at www.penguinputnam.com

The Library of Congress has catalogued the
G. P. Putnam's Sons edition as follows:

Davis, Max.
It's only a flat tire in the rain : navigating life's bumpy
roads with faith and grace / by Max Davis.
p.   cm.
ISBN 0-399-14692-X
1. Consolation.   2. Suffering—Religious aspects—Christianity.   I. Title.
BV4909 .M37   2001   00-032840
242'.4—dc21

Printed in the United States of America

10   9   8   7   6   5   4   3   2   1

Acknowledgments

Without the help of many extraordinary people a book like this has little hope of completion, much less of making it to the shelves of bookstores. First, I would like to thank my literary agent, Meredith Bernstein. Your hard work and extra time spent on this project will never be forgotten. You've made me a better writer and a better person. To Wendy Hubbert, my editor at Putnam: Thank you for believing in this project. It was a luxury to work with you from beginning to end. To Debbie Penny, my editor in Baton Rouge: Without your friendship and constructive criticism, I don't know what I would do. I've come to depend upon your insights. To Alanna, my life's partner: Your name should be on this book as co-author, because you gave each chapter the balance it needed. And finally, I would like to thank Jesus Christ, my best friend, for turning my life around and making it possible for me to live my dream.

To my three radiant stars:
Kristen, James, and Treva

Kristen, you never cease to amaze me with your intrinsic ability to see the positive in tough situations. Your high energy, work ethic, and love of life are contagious. You, my child, can be a world changer.

James, your compassionate heart, winning personality, and incredible sharpness will take you far. I'm your father, but in so many ways, you have been my teacher.

Treva, my little toot-toot: Life would be incomplete for me without your singing around the house and addictive daily hugs. You are a gift to my life.

Contents

Introduction

Disappointment, adversity, frustration, and pain: they affect us all. They are a universal language. There's not a human being alive who hasn't felt the winds of adversity blowing hard at some time or another in his or her life. As a former pastor/counselor and now an author who speaks to people from all walks of life, I regularly come in contact with people in crisis. Here are just a few of the issues people have come to me about in the last few months:

> ~ A young man dives into a shallow lake, damaging his spine. He's now a quadriplegic stuck in a nursing home with mentally ill people. Though he is physically disabled, mentally he is sharp as a tack. He wants me to help him get out of the nursing home and into a place where he can live life with dignity and respect.

~ A man in his seventies has just lost his wife of over fifty years. They began their romance as childhood sweethearts. Now he feels lost and lonely. He just wanted to talk.

~ A man in his thirties, married with a young daughter, is struggling in his career. His family is deep in debt, and there never seems to be enough money. He came to me for advice.

~ A man, thirty-eight, with a beautiful wife and two little girls, has just found out he has cancer. He asks for prayer.

~ A woman called and asked if I would go talk to her daughter whose boyfriend was killed in an automobile crash. After six months, the daughter still can't seem to shake her grief.

~ A woman whose thirteen-year-old daughter had drowned in the bathtub after having a seizure wanted to meet with me to talk about writing a book. She felt she had learned deeply from the experience and wanted to share her insights with others.

~ A dentist wrote me a letter and said that she had reached an all-time emotional low and was asking God to please show her what to do. She said she told God she was sorry if He was sending her messages that she didn't understand. She wanted to tell me that she's found my last book to be a help and a comfort to her.

I could go on, but you get the point. Adversity is as much a part of the human experience as the sun rising in the east and setting in the west. Joseph Parker, one of history's great ministers, once said to a group of young seminary students: "Preach to the suffering and you will never lack a congregation. There's a broken heart in every pew."[1] I have personally found that statement to be true. People everywhere in the world today are struggling.

There is now a popular volume out titled *Don't Sweat the Small Stuff, and It's All Small Stuff.* This is a cute book, with some timely advice. But the truth is, life's ordeals are not all small stuff. Sometimes, even when we are doing the best we can, in a matter of seconds, we can find ourselves in the midst of brutal struggles that leave us feeling as if life were beating us up. Accidents occur. Loved ones get sick. People do things that hurt us. We make mistakes. Stock markets crash. No matter how much we plan, or prepare, or use prevention, adversity still finds a way to surprise us. Some of these misfortunes are small but frustrating, like having a flat tire in the rain on the way to an important event. Others are not so small, like cancer or domestic abuse.

But no matter how severe your trial or how deep your pain, *there is hope!* You need not be defeated by anything. Don't sink into the mire of despair. Your life can be a beautiful experience. You can turn your *adversity into opportunity,* your *tragedy into triumph,* your *hurt into happiness,* your *outrage into outreach,* and your *disappointment into reappointment.* I know, because I've seen it happen in myself and in others. Many of the troubled people I've spoken with have become the greatest sources of inspiration for me and for others I counsel. They've shown me that, yes, our troubles can be stepping-stones to growth and fulfillment.

This is not a book of theory. It was developed in the trenches of everyday life, and its principles are tried and true. My goal is not to offer canned answers to life's problems or trite formulas for overnight success, but to provide you with tools that will help you find *empowerment* and *peace* in the midst of difficult circumstances.

1.

When Life Happens

Crises bring us face-to-face with our inadequacy and our inadequacy in turn leads us to the inexhaustible sufficiency of God.

—CATHERINE MARSHALL

"DEAF!"... I sat there stunned. Numbness came over me. Then, as the word began to sink into my being, all sorts of emotions ran through my mind. "James can't be deaf!" I shouted at the doctor. At that time, all I knew of deafness was those people who chased me down in the supermarket parking lot, handing me cards that said "I'm deaf; please help me by buying a key chain." I always felt sorry for them.

"I assure you your son is deaf," the doctor replied. "We'll need to run more tests to determine the severity of his deafness. But he is deaf."

On this day, when my ex-wife and I found ourselves in the hospital with James, my life would change irrevocably. James was thirteen months old. Up to that point he seemed like a normal toddler, walking, cooing, laughing. But he had not started talking yet. It seemed to me that he should have at least been forming syllables. When I commented about James's not talking yet, people usually told me not to worry, that a boy's speech sometimes develops a little more slowly than a girl's. These thoughts put me at ease because I didn't want to think anything was seriously wrong with my wonderful little boy. Plus, James had been getting regular checkups and had always come back with a clean bill of health.

Then, at church one day, James's nursery worker told me I might need to get his ears checked because she had called his name and he hadn't responded. His mom and I agreed and made an appointment to see a specialist. We were expecting to hear the doctor say, "James has an infection. Take this antibiotic and come back in two weeks." So you can imagine our shock when he said, to my utter disbelief, "I'm sorry, but your son is deaf."

Further tests revealed that James is profoundly deaf. Which means, for all practical purposes, he has *no* hearing. He might pick up certain low tones but only if magnified to around 120 decibels. That's about as loud as a jet engine at takeoff. And even then, he hears only certain tones, not complete sounds, the way you or I do. Hearing aids do not help him much.

Leaving the doctor's office, I felt as if the weight of the whole world had been dropped onto my shoulders. My ex and I drove directly to our pastor's house. He and his wife sat with us on their sofa as we wept. Later that night, at home, I sneaked up behind James and yelled at the top of my lungs—no response. He never knew I was there. I wept more. I wept for days.

God answers prayer. I believe that. I've seen it happen in dramatic ways. But when I prayed for James, all I felt was a cold silence. Others offered prayers on his behalf. Whole *congregations* offered prayers. Still, no response. For weeks I clanged pots and pans around James, hoping for some response, some sign—but nothing. Pain and guilt dominated my emotions. Maybe we could have caught his condition before it was so profound. Realizing that James would never hear my voice, or the sound of a bird chirping, or music playing made my chest feel as if it were going to explode with pain. Playing the guitar and singing were passions of mine. Now all motivation for performing music left me. How could I play when James could never share that with me?

Basically, in one afternoon, my whole family was thrust into a world we had no desire to enter—the deaf world. Stepping into this world forced me to confront issues and problems I didn't want to deal with. It meant years of sign language classes for all of us. James had to be enrolled in a special school at the age of eighteen months because a child's first five years are believed to be the most formative.

Once, in preschool, James was placed in a special-education class that included a teacher for the hearing impaired. When I went to visit him, they had him in class with the mentally disabled. I have nothing against the mentally challenged, but James's mind is fine. He just can't hear. I marched down to the school board and demanded that they place him in another school. Back came the pain—more weeping. As much as I wanted my son to hear, I was powerless to control the situation. My son was deaf, and I had to accept that fact.

Eleven years have passed since then. It's been a tough eleven years. Experts say that raising one deaf child is equivalent to raising seven hearing children. The typical thing to write would be: "Oh, over the years I've come to see deafness as a wonderful thing, and life is great now." The truth is, I *still* struggle with James's deafness. Each day brings new challenges. I often feel inadequate to father him. The pain of his situation is still an ever-present reality. I would give up my hearing in a split second if it meant James would receive his. I tell the truth.

Another truth I can tell is *There is hope!* Our hope lies *not* in our ability to prevent adverse events from touching our lives, or in our ability to control circumstances, but rather in the fact that we *can* have peace during tough times and we *can* transcend these periods, regardless of their intensity. Webster defines *transcend* as "to rise above." Notice that transcend does not mean "eliminate." Trials will always be a part of the human experience. They come to us in a myriad of fashions, all at different levels. Yet, the principles for transcending trials and experiencing peace within them are the same.

PRINCIPLE #1

Understand That Life Is a Struggle

This is a hard thing. It's hard because we want to control life. We want life to be painless. We don't want to struggle.

We want a "normal life." The difficulty is that everyone's definition of normal is different. In our materialistic society, we are constantly bombarded with images that impose unrealistic expectations upon us. They tell us that in order to be happy we must have this thing, or live in that house, or look like a supermodel, or be married to a supermodel, or live in the suburbs with two beautiful kids and have a marriage with no problems, etc. . . .

Many people's image of a "normal life" is a smooth ride. Hollywood-type ideals leave us believing that a normal life is filled with excess—that if we have problems, we are abnormal or we did something to deserve them. We fall into the trap of comparing our lives to others', often oblivious to their own personal struggles. For the most part, we see only the surface of others. But underneath the surface, most of them are struggling, too.

We find ourselves on a quest, driving toward the way we think life should be. And when adversity hits or our plans don't pan out, we sometimes feel cheated, as if this were *not* normal. Which leads me to the question, "What is a normal life?"

Scott Peck wrote in *The Road Less Traveled:*

> *Life is difficult. This is a great truth, one of the greatest truths. It is a great truth because once we truly see this truth, we transcend it. Once we truly know that life is difficult—once we truly understand and accept it— then life is no longer difficult.*[2]

A "normal life" is one of much adversity and struggle, plain and simple. As Peck said, it's difficult. Things happen out of our control. People sometimes choose to complain or become resentful because they believe that somehow life should not be this way—that their problems are the exception to life's rule. How many times have we heard or stated such words as "Nothing ever comes easily for me"?—implying that others don't experience setbacks as we do. Once a woman said to me, "All my life I've tried to do the right thing, and this is what I get." Her perception of how life *should be* was different from the reality she was experiencing. Somewhere she picked up the notion that if she did "all the right things," her life would be problem-free. As a result of this thinking, she saw herself as a *victim* of life. This is a tragedy that engulfs our society.

We begin to transcend and experience peace only when we see life as a series of struggles and then, instead of complaining about them, we set out to solve them. Armed with this attitude, our faith, prayers, and optimism become focused upon creating solutions. We cease seeing ourselves as victims of life and become conduits for giving life, regardless of the depth of our trials. *This is success in its purest form.*

PRINCIPLE #2

Embrace the Struggle

Once we understand that life is a struggle, we must put this knowledge into action by embracing the struggle. Please understand this is not a negative thing. I'm not talking about being fatalistic, nor am I saying you should allow yourself to be abused or be a doormat for others. If you can get out of a bad situation by making a wise decision, then do it.

But there are some situations that have to be walked through. I'm talking about being real. If you knew me personally, you would know that I am an eternal optimist. I am a faith-driven person. Embracing the struggle is an attitude. It simply means replacing the fear of pain with seeing the value in that pain. Obviously, no one in his right mind wishes for pain. But pain is a fact of life, and what we do with it makes all the difference.

Packaged with James's deafness has come much pain, but with the pain have also come many unexpected *blessings*. Personally, I've experienced a depth of character that could have come no other way except through this trial. *I'm* a deeper person. *James* is a deeper person. Pain and struggle will do that, if we allow it. The great abolitionist Frederick Douglass said, "Where there is no struggle, there is no growth." Strength and definition come to the bodybuilder as he increases the resistance in his workout routine. A little chick struggles to peck its way out of the egg; its struggle is being used to build the strength necessary for survival in the outside world.

One day I went by James's school to take him home early. Recess was in progress, and I could see him on the playground playing with other children. His school includes both hearing and nonhearing students. Off to the side was a little boy who was both blind *and* deaf. Teachers communicate with him by using sign language; he actually feels their hands as they sign. It is a truly remarkable sight to behold and a means of communication that requires a great deal of patience from both the signer and the signee.

My eyes teared up as I watched my son, the wall climber, the "Wild Thing," patiently and compassionately hand-signing to this deaf and blind child. It was precious as the boy tenderly felt James's hands, almost surprised by the fact that someone other than a teacher was taking time with him. After James finished signing, he gently turned the boy in the direction he needed to go and walked with him to his desired destination. In the background, sounds of children playing blended with balls bouncing and jump ropes skipping on concrete. Most of the hearing kids didn't even notice the boy. They were too busy playing. With only fifteen minutes of recess, time was a valued commodity. They had to squeeze every second out of it. Others avoided him because he was different or because they just didn't know how to communicate with a blind and deaf boy. Yet, James, at ten years of age, compassionately understood this boy's frustration and took time, *his highly valued recess time,* to communicate with him.

James wasn't embarrassed or too busy. He wasn't worried about what his friends thought. *He wasn't afraid to touch someone different.* Now that's depth! That's maturity—more than many adults have! And it has come because James, himself, has had to struggle. My temptation as a father is to try to remove the struggles from his life. I'm learning that this would be a great mistake. It is the *struggle* that has helped mold James into the compassionate person he is today. It is sometimes difficult to understand, but struggles have a way of instilling compassion and understanding in our hearts, if we allow them to. *As we embrace struggle, instead of resisting it, we grow.*

Trust God

*Meanwhile, where is God? . . . When you are happy,
so happy that you have no sense of needing Him, if
you turn to Him then with praise, you will be wel-
comed with open arms. But go to Him when your
need is desperate, when all other help is vain and
what do you find? A door slammed in your face, and
a sound of bolting and double bolting on the inside.
After that, silence . . .*

—C. S. LEWIS[3]

My sister is an audiologist. Recently she ran a hearing test
on an eighteen-year-old young man who had been deaf
since infancy. He told her, "I have been praying for years
that I would be able to hear. Now I think I'm hearing
some sounds." His faith and hope were high. He was
sure that tests would reveal that his hearing was beginning to be restored. But they showed no change. He was
just as deaf as he had ever been. When my sister broke
the news to him, tears of disappointment ran down his
cheeks. My sister, too, felt heartbroken. The young man's
mother said, "Don't worry about him. He'll be fine. He's
used to this."

Could you imagine being used to this type of disappointment? I'm sure, more than once, this young man
has asked, "Where are you, God?" "Why have you abandoned me?" "Have you not heard my prayers?" In my
mind, there's no doubt; he, too, has felt the cold silence
that C. S. Lewis described in the above quote.

Personally, I can't tell you how many times I've prayed for God to "fix" James's ears. I've prayed a multitude of times for direction on how to deal with him. "Is he getting the right education?" "Should he go to the deaf school or be mainstreamed with hearing kids?" "Is he learning to read properly?" James is twelve and cannot talk at all. "Is this normal?" "How far behind is he?" "What can we do to catch him up?" You get the picture. And when I say I prayed, I don't mean some five-minute poem, either! I've pleaded, cried out, wailed in anguish for direction only to hear nothing—to feel nothing—to feel as if I'm making decisions with no guidance. In some instances, circumstances actually got worse.

How, then, can I recommend that one principle for achieving transcendence and peace is trusting God? Especially when there are so many unanswered questions. Trust God? It sounds so simplistic, so childlike, and so naïve.

But I say trust God, because He *can* be trusted! Consider St. Paul. God spoke to him through a bright light on the road to Damascus. St. Paul saw many miracles firsthand. He was delivered supernaturally from certain death on countless occasions. And yet, God did not remove the noted thorn in his flesh: many scholars believe Paul suffered from poor eyesight. Regardless of what it was, several times Paul pleaded with God to remove his thorn and God responded, "My Grace is sufficient." In other words, God was saying He can be trusted, not always to keep adversity from entering our lives, but to *guide us through it*. Time has shown this truth to me. Many times, when things have seemed hopeless and I felt overwhelmed, God's light has broken through my darkness in surprising ways that assured me He was on the scene.

For example, James loves sports, and he's a good athlete. Because of his deafness, however, he requires extra attention. Most coaches have no idea how to communicate with the deaf, nor do they have the extra time to focus on one player. As a result, James has had to learn through observation of the other boys. Last summer I volunteered to coach a little league baseball team at the YMCA. I figured that because I knew sign language, I could sign to James and talk to the hearing kids at the same time. It would be no big deal. When I volunteered, I made a point not to tell anyone that James was deaf. It was important to me that James receive no special treatment and that he get an equal chance. James's sign-up sheet asked his age and grade. It asked nothing about deafness, and I didn't tell. When the first coaches' meeting came around, I again mentioned nothing about his deafness.

Baton Rouge is a relatively large city, and I did not know any of the other coaches, nor did they know me. At the meeting, we were given a roster of names. This was our predetermined team. My instructions were to contact the players' parents before a certain date and set up practice. After the meeting, I went home. That was it.

A few days after the coaches' meeting, I received a phone call from the YMCA's director. The call went something like this:

"Mr. Davis, this is Bill at the YMCA. We have two deaf boys that are looking for a team to get on. Would you be willing to allow them on your team?"

"How did you find out that my son was deaf and that I know sign language?" I responded enthusiastically.

Silence on the other end . . . "I didn't."

"Wait a minute. You had no idea that I have a deaf son and that I know sign?"

"That's correct."

"Then why did you call me?"

"I just picked your name from our coaches' list."

"Of course I will take them. This means we have three deaf kids on our team. James will be thrilled!"

As you can imagine, I could hardly contain my excitement. And the story gets even better. Later that week, I started calling the parents of the children on my predetermined roster. When I got to boy number thirteen, his mother warned me in a concerned fashion, "Now I want you to understand that Aaron is deaf and will require some special help." I about leaped out of my chair! We had eight teams in the YMCA. There were only four deaf kids in our entire league. And *all four ended up on my team!* All this without any orchestration—at least *human* orchestration.

Now, I've seen some occurrences in my time that one could call mere coincidences. But even the most die-hard skeptic would have to admit this one could hardly be dismissed as such. All four deaf kids in the league end up on the one team where the coach knows sign language. Come on!

The message that comes screaming back to me is this: Even though I don't understand *why* James is deaf, even though I badly want him to hear, even though I struggle, something bigger than me is going on. It is bigger than my limited understanding. Did God make James deaf? Ten years ago I would have answered a hearty "No!" Today, I'm not so sure. I do know that God allowed it.

Through his deafness, James has different gifts than if he were "normal." My simple point is: God knows *exactly* where James is, and He cares for James as much as I do. God took something as ordinary as baseball to show this to me. Peace comes to my heart when I simply trust in that. *We transcend our troubles and experience peace when we learn where knowledge and intellect end and trust and faith begin.*

As I mentioned earlier, being an author/speaker has allowed me the opportunity to visit with a wide range of inspiring people. Many of them have transcended struggles much more challenging than mine and are living incredible lives despite their pain. I take note of these people. Almost all of them, either consciously or unconsciously, are applying the three principles I've shared with you in this chapter. Let me share one of their special stories with you.

When I first met my friend Robin, she wanted to die. She is forty-five years old, and for over twenty years she has been plagued with the most serious form of kidney damage. Her condition had produced other problems such as cataracts and nerve damage to her limbs. The medication she was on caused unwanted weight gain.

Her body is frail, and she walks with a cane. But perhaps the worse side effect of her condition was her inability to maintain any lasting relationships with the opposite sex. Her lifelong dream was to get married and have children. Now it seems that will never happen. These problems all left Robin feeling tired and bitter.

Robin's doctor told her that because her medication was becoming less and less effective she would eventually have to go on dialysis. On numerous occasions, she confessed to me that she would rather die than go on dialysis. She told me she had no reason to live. "Why would I want to prolong a life I hate?" Robin contended.

I, of course, argued the point, yet there was no reasoning with her. For over two years, Robin and I dialogued about her condition. We debated about her gifts and talents. We debated about her past. We debated about God. Robin believed in God but was pretty upset with Him. She was honest about it, though. To her, God seemed cold and unconcerned. She had prayed to Him for her health. She had prayed for a certain relationship to work out. Both situations only worsened. "If God is so great," Robin argued, "why does He allow so much suffering in the world?"

Finally, the day came when Robin's doctor told her that if she did not go on dialysis, she would be dead in three months. Robin told me she was ready to die, and she was going to refuse the dialysis. She asked me to perform the eulogy at her funeral. We argued again. This time, though, I got pretty emotional with her. Instead of playing into her self-pity, I asked her to go ahead with the kidney dialysis and apply the three principles I've recommended in this chapter for at least six months. "If you don't see a dramatic change in your outlook, then make your decision," I said. "But give it at least six months." Please understand, I was recommending this as a friend, not as a professional therapist. Then I asked if I could say a prayer for her. I am an advocate of the power of prayer. She responded, "Sure, go ahead, but don't get your hopes up": a typical answer from Robin. Note that I was not trying to convert her to any religion.

I prayed a simple prayer: "Lord, in your own way, unique to Robin, reach down and get through to her that you love her and that she is precious to you and the world." That was it.

That night, before Robin went to bed, she said she had three thoughts on her mind: (1) "I have no reason to go through dialysis because my life is miserable"; (2) "I have made up my mind, I am not going through with this"; and (3) "I am wiped out physically, so I'm not going to work in the morning." She then fell asleep. When Robin woke up the next morning she said, "I was consumed by a consciousness that overwhelmed me. I don't know why, but I wanted to live! And I felt compelled to call the doctor right then."

She continued, "It is pretty obvious that God did something while I was sleeping. That He changed my mind. It had to be God because my mind was made up." She was compelled by this inner guidance to read a book that had been lying around her house for a long time— *You Can Be Happy No Matter What,* by Richard Carlson and Wayne W. Dyer. It helped her realize that she could *choose life,* regardless of how she felt.

Robin asked herself the question "Am I going to allow bitterness to destroy me, or am I going to let it go?" She then made a conscious decision to *throw away her victim mentality, to embrace the struggle, and to trust God.*

It has been over a year since that day, and Robin's life has changed dramatically. She is not the same person today. In fact, I am continually amazed when I am around her at the almost 180-degree turnaround in her life. Because it has been over a year, I know that Robin is not just on an emotional kick. She says, "Nothing about my life externally has really changed. Some people would even say things have gotten worse. Mr. Wonderful has not walked into my life. I spend twelve hours a week on dialysis. But internally I've changed a great deal. For the first time in my life I am happy."

She continues, "I'm now seeing that blessings are happening all around me, but until I opened up to them, I didn't recognize them. I've noticed that as I've opened up to receiving blessings, I have started to become a blessing to others around me."

Wow! What a transformation! Robin is not afraid of dying, but she's in love with living, despite her difficulties. She is *transcending!*

By the way, James and I played touch football this weekend. My wife was the quarterback for both teams. He beat me three touchdowns to two. We all survived.

2.

Beyond Understanding

In the presence of a loving parent there is security ... No voice is more reassuring, no love more unconditional and embracing ... These are the wondrous attributes that the Rabbis vested in God.

—RABBI DAVID WOLPE[4]

Hey, Daddy, look at my split! Daddy, did you see my cartwheel? Daddy, Daddy, watch this cheer!"

This has been going on for the past ten years, almost constantly. If anyone was ever born to be a cheerleader, it was Kristen, my teenager. As far back as I can remember, this has been her big dream. And for years she's been practicing—seriously practicing. To help her dream become a reality, I enrolled her in gymnastics and have taken her to the local high school football games so she could watch and learn from the cheerleaders.

At Kristen's school, a student can't try out for cheerleading until the end of the eighth grade, for the varsity squad the following year. Kristen anxiously counted down the years, months, and then the days until tryouts. Finally, the big week arrived. Kristen brimmed with confidence. In her mind, there was no doubt that she would make it. After all, this was her dream. She had practiced, and to her, life was fair. I, on the other hand, was not so sure. Almost a hundred girls were trying out, and only a handful would make the squad. Plus, most trying out were upperclassmen. My wife had been a dancer in high school and told me horror stories about the girls who were not chosen, how not making it crushed some of them.

"What if she doesn't make it?" I thought to myself. "It may crush her self-esteem." I started to worry. Then I started to panic. In my mind, I imagined the worst-case scenario—Kristen not making the team, coming home crying, dejected, and me having to explain to her that life doesn't always work out as we plan. I know it may sound trivial, but my heart was hurting for her. Really, I was a nervous wreck!

On the day of tryouts, I constantly checked my watch. I knew the approximate time when she would go before the judges, and as soon as I thought she had made it home, I called.

"Kristen, sweetheart, how'd you do?"

"Well, Daddy, I'm a little scared because they called

me back to cheer a second time. I won't know if I made it until Monday."

"Monday! Who are these people? Why are they torturing us?" I thought internally. But to Kristen I projected a calm, cool attitude. I tried to prepare her by telling her how Michael Jordan didn't make his junior-high basketball team and how he never gave up.

On Monday, my stomach was in knots the entire day. At precisely 3:30 P.M., I called to get the news. Eagerly, my fingers pressed the numbers on the phone. The phone was busy. My mind started to imagine the worst: "Maybe she didn't make the squad and is crying to her best friend." I pressed the numbers again. Still busy. One more time. Yes! It was ringing.

"Hello," Kristen answered.

"Honey, it's Daddy. Did you make it?"

"Yes, yes, I made it! I made it!"

"All right!" Relief! Joy! I almost did a cheer and back flip!

"By the way, Daddy, my uniforms and cheerleading camp are going to cost seven hundred dollars."

Gulp . . . Swallow . . . "Seven hundred what? . . . No problem, honey. I guess Daddy will take care of it. He always does."

Can you believe it? Not the seven hundred dollars, but me, a professional businessman, a macho ex–college football player, getting all worked up over some high school cheerleader tryouts. And I must confess, this cheerleader event was only one of many times I've gotten a bit worked up about my kids.

You should have seen me when James hit his first home run, and his second and third! I was jumping up and down like a fool, screaming so loudly that I later lost my voice.

The other day, Treva, my nine-year-old, and I were in line at the grocery store. She was holding a box of stationery and stickers, which I was buying for her. A woman in line next to us commented on her lovely items (we call them prizes). Treva nonchalantly remarked back to the lady, "I know. He spoils me." And it's true. I do. I can't help myself. I just want to give and give to my kids. I'm also incredibly protective of them. My motto is "You can mess with me, but you'd better not touch my kids, or I'll be touching you!"

When it comes to my children, all sorts of emotions run through my mind. I worry more. I hurt more. I laugh more. And the love. I didn't know this much love was possible. It's a love that's different from any other. It's a love that goes *beyond understanding*.

It all began for me the moment I held Kristen, my oldest, in my arms for the very first time. Once her sparkling eyes locked onto mine, there was no turning back. In that instant, something magical took place—something supernatural—something spiritual. In the twinkling of an eye, I was no longer just another guy; I was now a daddy. And it's daddies' job to do special things for their kids—to protect them, provide for them, teach them, and most of all love them. Don't get me wrong, now. I'm not trying to pat myself on the back or anything like that. When it comes to their kids, most parents, both moms and dads, do extraordinary things.

And though human parents make human mistakes, the unconditional love they have for their children comes from the source of all unconditional love—God.

All my life I have heard the words "God is love." And even though, while growing up, I wondered about pain in the world and had many questions directed toward God, I always believed that God loved me. I guess it was partly due to the fact that I had loving parents and they instilled in me at an early age that God is love. It may sound simple, but every time my mother put her arms around me, I somehow felt that she was an extension of God. I knew everything was going to be all right. When Daddy did things with me, like coming to almost every football game I ever played in, peewee through college, and protecting me when I did some pretty stupid things, I felt the security that every child needed to feel. My image of God was shaped, in large part, by my image of my parents. I knew God loved me and felt it through my parents. Our view of our parents directly affects our view of God. This can be positive or negative. If our parents were loving and caring, not necessarily perfect, our view of God will be a loving one. However, if our parents were abusive and unloving, our view of God will be negatively affected. We'll talk about that at the end of this chapter. For now, I want to focus on God as a loving, caring parent.

It wasn't until I became a parent myself that the full impact of God's love truly began to hit me. When I realized how much I love my own children, how this unconditional devotion to them flowed out from within me, I began to get a glimpse into the depth of God's love for humanity. *None of my children is perfect, but it doesn't matter. I don't love them because they are perfect; I love them because they're mine.* And God loves us because we are His.

In fact, God is our ultimate parent. When we understand Him as a complete, loving, and caring parent, with His unconditional affection aimed toward us, it directly affects how we relate to ourselves, others, the world, and Him. This understanding helps us to find empowerment during the difficult storms in our lives. A lost child wandering in the street has no direction, and soon fear begins to set in. But when the child's parents appear and take the child by the hand, instantly the anxiety and fear are replaced with peace, and a sense of empowerment sets in. The empowerment comes not from the child himself or herself, but from the fact that the child's parents are standing nearby. Understanding God, as our parent, gives us that same comfort.

When Jesus instructed his disciples to pray, he told them to begin by praying, "Our Father who art in Heaven . . ." The word *Jesus* used for "Father" is the Aramaic term *Abba.* This is a word, like *Daddy* or *Papa,* that small children once used for their fathers. Jesus was stressing an intimate way of addressing God. By calling God Abba, He was suggesting a relationship of the deepest intimacy—parenthood. When my children call me Daddy, they are using that name with all its privileges. "Daddy" means they can approach me. They can hop onto my lap. They can ride on my back. They can call out for me at night when they are scared. Those same privileges also apply to moms. This is what Jesus was trying to get across when he told his disciples to pray "Our Abba who art in Heaven . . ." Jesus was not trying to establish male supremacy but an intimate, parental relationship. David Ariel, president of the Cleveland College of Jewish Studies, wrote:

> *God is neither male nor female but exhibits what the rabbis must have seen as ideal characteristics of any parent: love, nurturance, empathy, placing the child's needs first, self-sacrifice, and self-restraint . . . God, like a parent . . . is both restrained and nurturing . . .*[5]

For a moment, let's consider some of the characteristics that make up both loving, caring parents and God's parental nature. Then we will see what wonderful possibilities exist for us when we apply these characteristics to our lives.

Good parents love their children unconditionally; God loves us unconditionally

The story of Bill* is a tough, but vivid, illustration of unconditional love. What for most dads is just a nightmare became a reality for Bill. His teenage son, Kenny, was found guilty of murdering his ex-girlfriend and her boyfriend. In a jealous rage, Kenny gunned down both of them in cold blood. No doubt this was a hideous crime for which there was no excuse. Everyone, including

---

*Names have been changed.

Kenny's parents, was stunned because Kenny had always seemed like such a good kid. He had lots of friends, made excellent grades in school, and was planning to attend medical school. Bill knew his son was guilty and was called to testify against him. Can you imagine the gripping pain this dad must have gone through in testifying against his own son?

On the witness stand, with tears streaming down his face, Bill told the jury the whole truth. Kenny was convicted on two counts of first-degree murder and sentenced to death by lethal injection. After the deliberations, the jury said it was Bill's testimony that had made the difference between his son's getting life in prison or the death penalty. In a nationally televised interview, Bill told the world, again in tears, that he felt his son had to pay for his crime. He explained the guilt and anguish he and his wife felt for the victims and their families.

Today, Kenny is on death row awaiting his execution. One would think that after his son had done such horrible things, his father would just write him off and try hard to forget he even existed. But twice a week, Bill visits Kenny in prison and is still interested in building a relationship with him. Kenny says he doesn't blame his dad for what he had to do. He realizes he is guilty and understands that he must pay for what he has done. Bill says that he is helping his son prepare for death. He plans to be by his side when Kenny takes his last breath. As heinous as Kenny's crime was, it could not keep his father from loving him.

God loves us in the same way. When we do things that we can't even forgive ourselves for, God is there for us. Yes, there are consequences to our actions—sometimes serious consequences. But God is ready to forgive and restore us if we allow Him to. I'm reminded of King David, who was known for his adultery with Bathsheba and for the eventual murder of Bathsheba's husband. There were serious consequences to David's actions. One consequence was the death of David's son. Yet, like a loving parent, God *unconditionally* loved David, reaching down to forgive him and eventually restoring him to a position of honor. Thankfully, we don't all commit murder, yet we all do fall short. It's what we *do* when we fall short that makes the difference. *The key is running to God when we mess up, not running away from God.*

Good parents hurt when their children hurt; God hurts when we hurt

Last month, my youngest daughter, Treva, had to undergo a root canal operation. She was a bit nervous. But I was terrified! Ten or so years ago, I had had root canal surgery, and the tooth was not completely deadened. You get the picture. More than once the dentist touched a nerve in my tooth and almost sent me through the ceiling. He responded to my anguish by nonchalantly saying, "I guess the anesthesia hasn't taken effect yet." Meanwhile, I thought I was dying! Before Treva's appointment, this scene replayed in my mind over and over.

Finally, when we arrived at the dentist's office, I asked her, "Honey, do you want me to hold your hand? I will be here for you if you need me." She said, "Sure," and acted as if it were no big deal. But I was so nervous for her that the dentist made me leave the room!

About an hour later, I went back to get her, and she was one big smile. The dentist remarked to me, "The kids always do better than the parents."

Why? Why is that statement true? It's because parents feel for their kids. They hurt for their kids. They would much rather be hurt themselves than allow their kids to feel pain. And this is how God feels about us. It may not seem like it, but God hurts when we hurt.

Even though God hurts when we hurt, He sometimes knows that to intervene would cause us greater pain down the road. This principle was driven home to me recently during an accident that involved James.

On Kristen's tenth birthday, the unimaginable happened. We were celebrating a normal birthday party. What could go wrong at a child's birthday party, right? Some relatives helped decorate. As a part of the decorations, they hung balloons all around the front porch. They were hung on nails that had been driven securely into the wood to hang potted plants. One of the balloons was the thick latex type, with a heavy-duty rubber band attached—the kind that you bounce back and forth off your knuckles while holding the rubber band. As the scenario unfolded, James wanted a balloon—not just any balloon, but that balloon. It was within his reach, so he grabbed it and did what any eight-year-old would do. He started pulling. But the rubber band was attached to the nail and wouldn't come down. The more James pulled, the tighter the rubber band stretched. Then, in a microsecond, the nail, not the balloon, was dislodged. The force of the stretched rubber band bulleted the nail directly into James's chest, embedding it there. You can imagine our shock as James came stumbling into the living room, stunned, with a three-inch nail driven into his chest!

It was not a pretty sight. The nail had projected through his bone and was driven so deep that we thought he might die. We were scared to move him because we didn't know if the nail had hit an artery or a lung or what. Someone called 911. Soon an ambulance and fire truck filled our front lawn. Lights were flashing everywhere. Cars were slowing down on the street to inquire. Kristen's birthday cake and presents lay untouched as the paramedics worked intensely. The girls were crying. The paramedics secured James so he could not move, slid him into the ambulance, and whisked him away as my father-in-law and I followed. They would not allow me to ride in the ambulance with my own son. James watched in terror, screaming for me to come, but all I could do was watch. What must have gone through his mind during that ambulance ride? "Why has Daddy left me? Why won't he come?"

At the hospital, the X rays revealed that the nail had barely missed an artery and was resting on his lung. Mercifully, it had not punctured it. The ER doctor's words went like this: "It is evident that someone upstairs is watching over your son, because if that nail had lodged a half-inch in either direction, he could be dead. Also, the nail could have hit his eye or gone into his head." Then the doctor told me, "We could put him under anesthesia and do surgery to remove the nail, but for someone as young as James, that might cause further complications. We need to get the nail out now." Then he looked at me and said, "It's going to be painful. But it's for the best."

James was given pain medication, but it had little effect and he was screaming. The doctor instructed me to hold my son down while he attempted to remove the nail. Soon we realized that this was going to be a much more difficult task than we had first thought.

Each time the doctor merely touched the nail, the pain would send James jerking and screaming. The doctor took a pair of pliers and started pulling the nail, but it wouldn't budge. It was driven in his chest like a nail hammered into a piece of lumber. The whole time James's eyes were locked onto mine. They piercingly said it all: "Daddy, do something. Don't let the doctor hurt me. Please, Daddy, please." I too was in tears and, in a moment of weakness, let go.

The doctor sternly confronted me and said I had to be strong and hold him down. "It is for James's own good," he reminded me. Despite knowing what was best, holding my son down was one of the hardest things I've ever had to do. I also knew that I had within me the authority to stop the whole procedure and request surgery. My instincts as a father, however, told me that this was the best way in the long run. So, I took a deep breath and, once again, wrapped my arms around James and held him down—this time more tightly than before. The whole time his eyes never stopped speaking to me:

"Dad, how could you betray me, you of all people. I trusted you. You know how this is hurting me. Daddy, I'm in pain. Do something." Yet, all I could do was hold him down. This time, the doctor literally straddled James and pulled with his arms using his legs for more power. That's how deeply lodged the nail was. Finally, after what seemed an eternity, the nail popped out. James and I sat there, in a pile of sweat, exhausted and emotionally spent. The pain subsided. The distress was over. James looked at me, as if to say "Daddy, why did you let them do that to me?" All I could do was hold him in my arms and love him. He couldn't understand why I had done what I did, and words wouldn't matter. "When he gets older and more mature," I thought, "then he will understand."

The bottom line is: Yes, my son was hurting. Only another parent can know the torment I was going through. And just as God has the power to step into our lives and say Enough is enough, I too had the power to stop James's pain. Yet, I knew to do so would be more harmful to him. I was hurting for my son. God hurts for us.

"The Lord is close to those whose hearts are breaking"
(Psalm 34:18).

Good parents give loving boundaries; God gives loving boundaries

James wants a motorcycle. He reads motorcycle magazines. He has motorcycle posters in his room. Every time we drive by a motorcycle shop, he wants to stop and look. For the past three Christmases he has asked for a motorcycle. Do you think he's got one? Not on your life!

Do you know why? Because I know James better than he knows himself. Even though he thinks he's ready, I know he's not. Sometimes he gets mad at me because I don't give him what he wants, but I am protecting him from himself. I had a friend who, in his midtwenties, was killed on a motorcycle, and he was a responsible person. I also know of a young girl who had to have her leg amputated because of a motorcycle crash. I'm not saying I'm against motorcycles, but as a parent, I can't give my son something I know he can't handle. Loving boundaries, set by loving parents, are what give a child protection. *Loving boundaries, set by a loving God, are what give us protection.*

The reason we have moral laws (boundaries) in the universe is not because God is a big, bad god and wants to make our lives miserable. God loves us and wants what's best for his children. Rabbi Stewart Vogel, commenting on the Ten Commandments, said, "People may feel intimidated by God's laws because they just see them as a list of rules that one must live by or else, but underlying these rules are the most important concepts of love, honor, and respect."[6] God has placed, deep within the soul of each human, those universal laws, and I believe we all inherently know them.

These universal laws transcend religions and culture. Consider the following examples of moral laws, as believed in by different civilizations throughout history.

Even though these civilizations rose independently from one another, the similarities among their laws are striking.

"Slander not" (Babylonian).

"Thou shalt not bear false witness against thy neighbor" (ancient Jewish).

"Utter not a word by which anyone could be wounded" (Hindu).

"Never do to others what you would not like them to do to you" (ancient Chinese).

"Do unto others as you would have them do unto you" (Christian).

"A sacrifice is obliterated by a lie and the merit of alms by an act of fraud" (Hindu).

"The gentleman must learn to keep his promises" (ancient Chinese).

"Do not lie to each other" (Christian).

"Honor thy father and mother" (Judeo-Christian).

"To care for parents" (Greek).

"Your father is an image of the Lord of Creation; your mother is an image of the Earth. For him who fails to honor them, every work of piety is in vain. This is the first duty" (Hindu).

"You will see them take care of their old" (Native American).

These are just a few of the hundreds of similar laws contained in all the world's cultures. This is so because God has placed within each and every person the universal laws of His nature. It's part of being created in God's image. Acts 10:34–35 in the New Testament plainly says, "... God does not show favoritism, but accepts men from every nation who fear him and do what is right." Many people choose to live by God's guidelines the best way they can, and others may choose not to. But when we go outside of God's intended plan, we often get hurt, and most of the time others get hurt as well. God's desire is to protect and provide for His children. This is why He gives us loving boundaries to follow.

On a personal level, God knows each one of us better than we know ourselves. Sometimes when we pray for things that God knows are not best for us, the answer is no. I am reminded of the song by Garth Brooks, *I Thank God for Unanswered Prayers*. In this song he prays earnestly for God to restore a broken relationship, but God does not answer his prayer. The relationship ends. Several years later, however, after Garth marries and has a child, he happens across his old girlfriend and instantly realizes how much he loves his family and what a mistake it would have been if this other relationship had not ended. In the song, Garth falls on his knees and cries out, "I thank God for unanswered prayers."

I love that song. The only thing I might change would be the fact that God did answer Garth's prayer. The answer was "No, Garth. Trust me. I have something better for you."

Good parents give good things to their children; God gives good things to us

It took me the longest time to realize that God wants good things for me. He is not out to get me. Nor is He against my succeeding and being happy. In fact, God is about *abundant life.* Just look at nearly all parents during the holiday season. They have their lists and pack their shopping carts, trying desperately to get their children what they want. Money may be tight, but these loving parents do whatever it takes—beg, borrow, or steal!

If a loving parent can't provide for his children, he will humble himself to extraordinary levels in order to see his children's needs met. I'll never forget the Christmas of '97. I was signing books at a store in Nashville. The weather was absolutely horrible. It was cold, and raining cats and dogs. Wind whipped through the parking lot, pushing rain and bursts of freezing air into the store each time the automatic doors opened.

Needless to say, very few people showed up for my signing. In fact, the store was practically empty. But that night was one of my more memorable book events. A young lady braved the elements. She came in soaking wet, shivering, with smeared makeup. She was also crying. When I asked what was going on, she launched into a horrible story of spousal abuse. Her husband was on drugs and alcohol, and beat her and their children. He spent all their money on his habits, leaving nothing for Christmas. She was desperate. I knew her story was authentic; she never asked me for money. Instead, she simply handed me a piece of paper with a list on it. I remember that list well.

- Kelly, 12 years old, size 14 pants, 6 shoe, wants a Hot Wheels set

- Allan, 16 years old, size 28 pants, 10 shoe, wants a Sony Walkman

- Eight-month-old baby—needs warm clothes

- Could use some food for Christmas dinner

At the bottom of the list, she had written her address and phone number. I gave her a copy of my book and told her I would help. When I meet people like this, my policy is to operate through a qualified organization. She thanked me and left with what dignity she had left. I soon called a local church, which made sure this woman's family was taken care of. Wow! What a mom! This mother loved her kids enough to humble herself in order to see them taken care of.

And to think, God loves us just that much! Nothing can separate us from the love of God. Nothing.

I know it's a travesty the way we overspend and give our kids too much. Truthfully, we should cut back. But we don't. We don't cut back because we want to see them smile. When our children are happy, we feel this deep sense of satisfaction. Of course, we all know that you can't buy love or happiness, but still, we like showering our kids with gifts.

Four years ago, Kyle donated one of his kidneys to his dying daughter, Missy. His special gift gave Missy new health and hope. However, at the time of this writing, the kidney is failing, and she has had little success finding another donor. Missy could possibly receive a kidney from an unrelated person with similar blood characteristics, or even from a cadaver, but related donors greatly increase the success potential of a transplant. Her dad, Kyle, was determined the *only* suitable relative. Doctors now say that unless Missy receives a new transplant, she will surely die. She is just sixteen years old.

Because Kyle loves his daughter unconditionally, he has offered to give Missy his remaining kidney. This would save his daughter but would place his own health in serious jeopardy since he would have to go on dialysis. Missy's doctors at the University of California at San Francisco first balked at the transplant request, but an ethics panel is reviewing the matter at the urging of her family. Kyle's unusual offer, which would have to be approved, raises questions about whether it is acceptable for someone to sacrifice his own future for the future of his child through organ transplantation. "We were told it would be unethical," said Missy's mother. But another source said, "We believe it's not about ethics. These are family members making a decision for the future of their child."

The ultimate gift loving parents can give is the gift of themselves. Think about it. *"If we, being human, desire to give good things to our children, how much more does our Heavenly Father delight in giving good things to His children?"* (Matthew 7:11).

Good parents are not overprotective; God is not overprotective

An overprotective parent can be just as harmful as a parent who gives no protection. Good parents recognize the need to let their children go out on their own. Good parents guide and suggest and sometimes intervene, but as a whole, there comes a time when children have to be released, even if releasing them may cause them harm and pain. Good parents have to let go. Letting go is part of love. *Control is not love.*

God chooses not to control us. One of the unique characteristics of being human and created in God's image is our freedom to determine our own destiny, as both individuals and as a species. Freedom of choice is one of the most precious gifts God has bestowed upon mankind. God knew that without choice or free will there could be no reciprocal love. Without free will, man would be no different from animals. Animals are programmed. They have instinct. But humanity has the ability to choose. Humankind can think, reason, and love. But we can also hate, hurt, and destroy. We have knowledge of good and evil. We possess a plethora of emotions that animals don't have. We can feel grief, frustration, jealousy, betrayal, hatred, love, joy, hope, and creativity.

God knew that in order to love us fully He had to release us. This release was necessary for us to have the chance to love God in return, since choice is the foundation of a relationship. God also knew that in order to create love, the possibility of evil and suffering would enter the world. Yet God loved us so much that He still chose to give us choice.

When we find ourselves in difficult and painful situations, it is important to know that God did not cause these situations and that He hurts with us. He doesn't want to see us suffer any more than a loving parent wants to see his child suffer. Sometimes God intervenes by interrupting the natural laws set in the universe—through what we call a miracle. I believe in miracles, yet, I also believe it's possible, because of God's infinite justice, that for Him to intervene would mean going against His bigger plan for humanity. Sometimes, especially when a child is grown, a parent wants desperately to intervene in the child's life but knows all too well that doing so could, in the long run, cause more harm than good. A good parent lets go but is always waiting there with open arms if called upon. *Though God may not always intervene as we want Him to, He is always there, like a loving parent, for us to run to and receive the strength and power we need to continue on and to overcome.*

Our parents affect our view of God

Now, I realize that for many, seeing God as the ultimate parent may open up all kinds of issues. It is common to take the feelings we hold toward our parents and direct them toward God. Our view of God is often closely tied to our view of our parents. This can be good or bad.

For Marjorie Holmes, as she writes in *How Can I Find You, God?* it was good:

> *This dad, this earthy earthy father . . . looking back I find more pointers toward God in him than I realized. He was not complex, he was never remote. He was never too busy to listen to us. And though he sometimes got mad and yelled and was stern and we thought him unfair, we found out he wasn't. He was quick to forgive and he never held a grudge.*
>
> *He loved us, was concerned about us, and was proud of us. He never let any of us down, not once . . . What more can anyone ask of a father? And if this is the nature of a good earthly father, why shouldn't the father of us all be just as easy to know and to trust?[7]*

For some it is not so good. When thinking of their parents, images of abuse, pain, abandonment, shame, all come rising to the surface of their emotions. Or, it could be because their parent(s) has died or was killed, leaving them with a void. If this is the case, it is hard to picture God as a loving, caring parent. The blessed Mother Teresa wrote in *The Joy in Loving:*

> *Vast regions of the world are covered by spiritual deserts. There you will find young people marked by human abandonment, the result of broken relationships, which affect them to their very depths. Even*

when they are thirsting for a spiritual life, many of the young are afflicted by doubt. They are unable to place their confidence in God, to believe, since they have not found confidence in those to whom life had entrusted them. Separations have wounded the innocence of their childhood or adolescence. The consequences are skepticism and discouragement. What's the use of living? Does life still have any meaning?[8]

Another girl named Teresa offers hope to all those unfortunate souls who can relate to Mother Teresa's quote. Teresa had gone to church most of her life, yet God seemed unapproachable. She said, *"I thought of Him as the Big Policeman in the Sky, ready to punish, but never warm and caring. God to me was much like my own father."* Teresa's distorted view of God developed in part because of her abusive father. He resented Teresa's getting any attention and any money being spent on her. Once, when she was thirteen years old, her father came stumbling into her birthday party, stone drunk, and yelled, "You're ugly and stupid!" Then he sneered, in front of her friends, "Nobody could ever love you." As a result of that trauma, Teresa became a loner and felt that she didn't belong anywhere.[9]

For those people with broken hearts and crushed dreams, God can help. God wants to show you the kind of supernatural love and acceptance that only He can give. If your earthly parents let you down, God can fill the void. As Teresa says, *"It all changed when I found you, Lord. You accepted me just as I am warts and all. I felt I had come home when I found you!"*

Today, as I watched my children playing, an overwhelming sense of love rushed through my being. I knew in my heart that, without question, I would give my life for any one of them. My heart flooded with peace as I realized that my Heavenly Father loved me in that same way.

3.

Honest
to God

*I can't be honest with God until I'm first honest
with myself.*

—ANONYMOUS

For a moment, I would like you to journey with me to
a faraway place and time—to the ancient land of Uz,
around 1500 B.C.

Our time machine will be the Scriptures and a good
imagination. In the ancient land of Uz lived the biblical
character of Job. Some scholars believe Job was an actual
person; others believe the biblical story about him was a
fictional creation to help illustrate a point. Regardless,
the Book of Job is inspired by God, and its message offers
solace to many.

Job was wealthy, to say the least. His personal hold-
ings consisted of seven thousand sheep, three thousand

camels, five hundred yoke of oxen (a thousand total oxen), five hundred donkeys, a vast number of servants, and a large, healthy family.[10] This would mean that his land probably had to consist of a bare minimum of ten thousand acres and a huge estate to house his servants! In those days, oxen, camel, and donkeys were as much in demand as automobiles are today, so it's likely that Job had amassed his fortune from raising and selling these animals. Seven thousand sheep could supply a whole region with wool for clothing.

Business-wise, we could compare Job to a Bill Gates or a Sam Walton. He was as big as they get. According to Scripture, Job was "the greatest man among all the people of the east."[11] Yet, unlike many other wealthy people, he remained humble in heart, realizing that his success was a direct result of God's gracious blessings. Job was a righteous man. In other words, he obeyed God, was a loving, committed husband and father, and ethical in his business dealings. Job was doing "all the right things."

Then one day (don't you hate those days?) Job's life abruptly took a series of ill-fated turns. In rapid succession, bam, bam, bam, tragedy struck. First, bandits attacked and killed his servants working in the fields, stealing a large number of animals. Then an out-of-control wildfire burned up the sheep and fields they were grazing in. Another group of bandits formed three parties and stole all his camels, killing their caretakers in the process. And finally, a fierce desert storm blew his home down killing his family, leaving only his wife. In the midst of his grief, Job became weak and his skin broke out in boils! After the dust settled, Job found himself penniless, sick, and grief stricken. He had now experienced it all, from wealth, health, and happiness to financial ruin, sickness, and grief from the death of loved ones. Job had hit rock bottom. All this turmoil happened, I must add, completely out of his control.

Job's pain was so great that he cried out, *"If my anguish could be weighed and all my misery be placed on the scales! It would surely outweigh the sand of the seas. . . . I have no peace, no quietness, I have no rest, but only turmoil. . . . My eyes will never see happiness again. . . . Cursed be the day I was born"* (Job 3:1, 26; 6: 2–3). To say that Job was hurting is an understatement. The man was in pain.

And even though our trials probably haven't become elevated to the level of Job's, how many of us have experienced similar thoughts? You don't want to do anything. You sense you are wasting away. Your deepest wish is to be restored to your definition of normality and to find release. You want to move forward with life, yet somehow, you're trapped in a deep, dark, jagged pit of despondency. You've tried climbing out on your own, but your limbs, which represent your burdens, are so heavy. Sometimes you just want to let go and fall deeper into the pit. Giving up often seems easier than facing another day. And the future—*what* future? Your life is in limbo. You can't visualize hope or dreams—just pain. This was Job's lot. He was in agony, physically and mentally.

Then, right smack dab in the middle of all his suffering, when he thought things couldn't possibly get worse, they did. Three friends showed up at his tent to comfort him and offer their words of advice. Oh, boy. When Job's comforters tried to help, instead of feeling better, his pain intensified! Job responded to his comforters by saying, *"How long will you crush me with your words? . . . Will your long-winded speeches never end? Will you never get enough of my flesh?!"*[12]

I don't know about you, but, man, can I relate! When going through adversity, there are always those people who think they have the answers to our troubles. They're convinced it's their mission to comfort us with their often self-righteous, judgmental, and misguided wisdom. Sometimes they're direct, but more than likely they slip in a cutting remark here or a damaging comment there, oblivious to, or not caring about, the emotional damage they are causing.

Most of the time these comforters have no clue as to what is really going on in our personal lives, but they really think they are helping. Usually these people are sincere. Before bashing Job, one of his friends said, *"But now, Job, listen to my words. . . . My words come from an upright heart; my lips sincerely speak what I know."*[13] Then he began to tell Job what he had done wrong to have been so beset by misfortune and what he needed to do to recover.

Yes, Job's comforters were sincere. But, guess what? They were sincerely wrong! How do I know? In the end of the Book of Job, God doesn't rebuke Job for his pain or even his honest questions of God but, instead, rebukes Eliphaz, the leader of the so-called comforters, by saying, *"I am angry with you and with your two friends, because you have not spoken of me what is right."*[14] Even though the comforters were convinced they were speaking for God, they were not.

Job's comforters, at first, truly empathized with him. They were so overwhelmed by his condition that *"no one said a word to him, because they saw how great his suffering was."*[15] Then they cried alongside him for seven days. That's the best thing they did, and it was the right thing. People who are hurting don't need our lectures or sermons. They need our grace, hope, compassion, practical help, and support. Just being there and available to them is probably the greatest thing we can do: Become a support to lean on. Encourage those in pain to take one small step at a time, with small pictures of reality that are positive. Help them realize the success to be achieved in day-to-day tasks.

Job's friends empathized with him for a period of time. As time passed, however, and Job did not come around as quickly as they thought he should, their support turned to criticism. I can picture the scene vividly in my mind: One of Job's comforters may have said something like "Okay, Job, you've grieved, you've cried, now it's time to move on. It's time to snap out of it and pull yourself up by your bootstraps." When Job didn't respond to his friends' urgings, they began to try to *"fix"* him. The problem with Job at this stage, and with most people who are experiencing deep pain, is that they can't pull themselves up by their bootstraps. Job himself admitted this when he asked his comforters, *"Do I have any power to help myself? . . ."*[16] The implication was "No, I don't."

Healing takes time, and that's okay. Each individual person has his or her own timetable for restoration. This time isn't a license to give up and wallow in self-pity, but rather a time for cleansing. It is important to give sufficient time to the grieving process and let pain perform its function. If we don't grieve properly over a loss, we may carry guilt or bitterness or anger inside of us the rest of our lives.

Also, Job's friends assumed that because they were not suffering as Job was, they were somehow more upright and moral than he. Isn't it interesting how, when we are physically and mentally well and are experiencing success, we sometimes believe we are just a little better than those who aren't? As though we might be doing something right—we made all the right choices, and it's paying off. It's very subtle, but I assure you, we do it. When you find yourself thinking those thoughts, beware. You or someone you love may need some help and compassion one day.

Job had done nothing wrong, nor had he made any bad decisions. In contrast to the angry rebuke God gave Job's comforters, read what is written of Job himself: *"Job was blameless and upright . . . In all this (adversity), Job did not sin or charge God falsely . . ."*[17] Yet his friends were certain Job had screwed up. Then, to make a point, God told Job's friends to admit their *"folly"*[18] (God calls their know-it-all counsel folly!) and to get Job to pray for them. Talk about a slap in the face for Job's comforters—after all their pious words. After that, God told them that He would *"accept Job's prayer, because he has done what is right."*[19]

Just because we are experiencing painful situations in our lives doesn't necessarily mean we are doing something wrong or have a lack of faith. Our natural tendency, though, is to take on *"false"* guilt that is often magnified by others. Remember that there is a delicate balance between taking personal responsibility and taking on false guilt.

A dear friend of mine fought a long, hard battle against lung cancer for over two years. Eventually, the cancer got the best of him, and he died at the young age of fifty-five. During his bout with this ruthless opponent, he read Scriptures, prayed, stood by faith, and praised God. He was a man of deep faith. Yet, as the disease began to take a higher toll, he began to feel guilty. One night, in desperation, almost in a panic attack, he called me and sought assurance that God hadn't abandoned him. He felt he must be doing something wrong or he would be winning this fight. I tried to reassure him that God did love him and that the Scriptures plainly show that the storms of life come to both the just and the unjust. Stuff happens. Storms happen.

Not only had Job not done anything wrong; he also understood that the issue was between him and God and that his friends had no right to judge him. After one critical comment, Job told one friend, *"I have a mind as well as you; I am not inferior to you. If it is true that I have gone astray, my error remains my concern alone."*[20] In other words, "I can think for myself. Stop trying to think for me. And please don't comfort me!" Job accepted responsibility for his situation. He was willing to, and he did, examine himself. But Job also knew the difference between personal responsibility and self-mutilation. He knew his position before God, and he fell on God's mercy. Job had enough confidence and security to know his own heart. False guilt is an enemy that wants to push us over the edge so that we are immobilized by our mistakes, misfortunes, and pain. Though their comments were surely painful, Job let his friends' pieties roll off of him like water rolling off a duck's back. Then, after he settled the issues with his so-called comforters, he directed his attention to a heart-to-heart dialogue with God. This is important. *Job knew whom* not *to listen to, but he also knew absolutely whom* to *listen to—God.* He also knew that God was listening to him. In his heart-to-heart with the Almighty, Job unloaded all his questions, doubts, fears, anger, and frustrations on God. Job was not afraid to be honest with God!

How about you? What's your trauma? Have you lost your job or a loved one? Are you handicapped? Divorced? Single? Disappointed? Betrayed? Do you feel as if you have been ripped off by life? Do you secretly entertain questions directed at God that you are afraid to ask out loud for fear of seeming faithless, unspiritual, cynical, or even blasphemous? Are you bitter at someone or some circumstance in your life? Do you feel the way Job did—as if you are all alone, yet surrounded by many inspecting eyes?

Most of us have been taught through the years never to question God. To do so means a serious lack of faith. After all, we have been told, "God works all things for our good to those that love Him." Or, "God is using all our hardships for the purpose of refining us." Now, don't misunderstand me. I fervently believe these statements are true. There is hope in God. God is our only hope. Sometimes, though, it is difficult to discern the "good" that is happening in those who have died of cancer, or have been involved in fatal accidents, or are seriously handicapped, etc.... To the person who is tragically hurting, Scriptures and slogans initially appear superficial or removed from the real issues of the heart. The story of Job affirms this. His so-called comforters' theological and psychological arguments actually *defended* God. They sounded right-on. They made good points, each with an element of truth in it. Let me paraphrase some of the half-truths they pointed out to Job as he agonized:

༄ *"Shhh, Job. Don't say such things! God doesn't like that. Only speak positive faith statements."* Positive confession is fine. I personally believe it can transform a life. But stuffing our true feelings can produce false guilt, leading us to think that God is displeased if we don't say the "right things" rather that being open and honest with Him. Besides, God knows our feelings anyway. Doesn't He? He's God. Honesty before God is for our benefit, not God's.

༄ *"Search your heart, Job. You must have some hidden sin. God rewards us for righteousness and punishes us when we deserve it. Job, if you will confess your sin and correct your ways, God will restore you."* Although bad things do happen because we do sin, false guilt comes when we believe God is punishing us every time something bad happens. Jesus plainly said, *"In this life you will have trouble. But take heart! I have overcome the world."*[21]

ↄ *"God is trying to teach you something, Job. Learn from this. You should feel honored, not angry. Remember to praise God in the midst of this."* Though each trauma we go through can ultimately be an opportunity for growth, comments like these lead us to believe that if we don't respond in a certain way, if the praises don't automatically flow out, that we are displeasing God or have a lack of faith. They also imply that God delights in putting us through painful trials just to teach us something. Nothing could be further from the truth. We experience most of our trials simply because we live in a mixed-up, crazy, fallen world. Of course God uses these things to teach us, but God also hurts when we hurt. I love the words of the late Roy Hicks, Jr.: "God has not given up on you even though you have yet to lift your voice in praise about the painful drubbing that has happened to you. God has not abandoned you. He's not docking you for not being someone else."[22]

ↄ *"God helps those who help themselves, Job."* This comment also seems rational and good. The problem is that often we can't help ourselves. We might need more time, and more support, and sometimes even professional counseling. But what we absolutely can't handle in those times of pain is critical judgment.

All these points brought forth by Job's comforters sounded right and good in themselves, yet *even God rebuked them!* God corrected these people for saying good things about Him. I want you to get this point: Just because an argument may be sound, or even correct, doesn't mean it's the right thing to say to the person in pain. Job's response to the points made by his comforters was *"I have heard many things like these; miserable comforters are you all!"*[23] Job had already heard it. He knew all the religious jargon. It wasn't anything new. It just wasn't helping him any. Concerning Job's comforters, Philip Yancey, in his book *Disappointment with God,* wrote, "The book of Job plainly shows that such 'helpful advice' does nothing to answer questions of the person in pain. It was the wrong medicine, dispensed at the wrong time."[24]

Frequently, the pressing issue if you are in pain is not whether God is making you stronger or working this out for your good, but rather, how do you deal with these lingering questions about God that challenge the very core of everything you believe. "How can I ever trust God again?" "God, where are you?" "Why even pray?" "God, if you are so good, how could you allow this to happen?" "What do I do with this anger and humiliation?" The questions are endless. And the pain? It immobilizes us.

I remember vividly the first year after I had experienced a devastating divorce following twelve years of marriage. I was pastoring a church at the time, doing God's work, and thought everything was fine. Then one day, just like that, I came home to an empty house. Overnight, my life radically changed. I was separated from my children, out of a home, and emotionally devastated. No one in my family had ever gone through a divorce, until me, and I was a pastor, of all people. The emotional pain was so excruciating that sometimes I would ball up in a corner and just cry. Once, while traveling at night, I pulled my car onto the shoulder of the road and paced up and down the interstate crying out to God. When the pain subsided somewhat, I got back in the car and moved on. Because I was so emotionally shattered, I resigned from the church. How could I counsel others when I couldn't handle my own problems?

For over a year, my relationship with God consisted of my calling out, "GOD!!! Help!!!" I wasn't saying all the right things, believing all the right things, or doing all the right things. Heck, I couldn't set foot in a church for over a year. It was too painful. The only thing—I mean, the only thing—that sustained me during that time was crying out to God honestly. Sometimes my faith wavered. I had many hard questions. Yet, God never let me go, even when I wanted to let go. And the friends who comforted me the most were those who were simply there for me. They didn't try to judge me or fix me. They just let me lean on them or opened their homes to me. For them, I am eternally grateful. The ones who did try to preach to me meant well, but they didn't help me much. It wasn't that what they were saying was wrong; it's just that I was in so much pain that nothing but the pain really mattered much.

The good news in all this is that God is faithful. He saw me through. It's been eight years, and I can honestly say I am happier than I've ever been, and I actually thank God for that painful experience. But when I was going through it, well, that was a different story.

The other day, while sitting in the steam room at the health club I attend, I struck up a conversation with another man. In the course of our conversation, he told me that a few years earlier he had lost a son to a drunken driver. Then he said, "Let me tell you something. It's not natural for a parent to bury his kid. It's supposed to be the other way around." I told him I couldn't imagine losing a child and asked how he makes it through life. His response wasn't deep and theological. It wasn't pretty and pious, but it was real. He said, "Man, every morning when I crawl out of bed, I fall on my knees and beg God to give me enough strength to make it through another day. And you know what? He has. One day at a time. I couldn't make it without the Lord's help."

One of the overwhelming messages of the story of Job is that *it's okay to dump on God all your questions, doubts, anger, guilt, grief, or whatever. God can handle it.* God wants you to be honest with Him. The thing God doesn't want us to do is block Him out—to ignore Him and turn within ourselves. God desires a relationship with us. And a healthy relationship has honest communication.

Job was in intense pain. He had honest questions and complaints, but he took them to God. Job asked God, *"Does it please you to oppress me, to spurn the work of your hands, while you smile on the schemes of the wicked?"*[25] Can you hear the sense of injustice Job felt toward God? Job was dreadfully honest in his pain. Yet, in that honesty, he also knew and trusted that God was still his only hope. He said, *"I know that my Redeemer lives. . . . Yet, will I hope in him. . . . Indeed, this will turn out for my deliverance."*[26]

Finally, after Job's comforters had raised all the arguments and Job had aired his complaints and confidences to God, God arrived on the scene in a whirlwind. God began to question Job: *"Where were you when I laid the earth's foundations?... Does the hawk take flight by your wisdom?... Does the eagle soar at your command? Who instills in the eagle the instinct to build its nest?..."*[27] In other words, "I am God, Job. You are not." Job's final response to God was, *"Surely I spoke things I did not understand, things too profound for me to know. I ... repent in dust and ashes."*[28] Job very much needed to air his frustrations to God. It was healthy. Yet, he ultimately recognized that God was not obligated to give him all the answers to his questions. Likewise, we will not always have clear black-and-white answers to our questions. And that's okay. As humans, we now only understand in part. We see through a glass dimly. But one day we shall understand fully.

Despite Job's honesty with God during his suffering, in the end God commended him while his comforters were rebuked. Why? Because even in his anger and frustration, even when he questioned God, Job communicated honestly with Him. The comforters, on the other hand, uttered many correct and impressive statements. Job talked directly to God; they only talked about God.

After writing this chapter, I was compelled to have a heart-to-heart talk with the Creator. How about you?

4.
Two Quarters of Grace

Guilt exposes a longing for Grace.
—PHILIP YANCEY

They, whoever they are, have said, "Never cry over spilled milk." That's fine. I can handle spilled milk. No problem. Just grab a rag and wipe it up. Simple enough. Right? But what about spilled gasoline? A five-gallon can—emptied out, exhausted, soaked up into the carpet of your van! Fumes so strong you think you're going to pass out. With one spark, the whole thing could go up in flames. Do you know how much gasoline five gallons is? As I found out for myself one recent summer, five gallons is a whole lot. Enough gasoline to ruin your customized van. Oh, I mean, your parents' customized van! Here's a quick lesson for you: Never borrow anything from anybody. It's much better just to do without.

Up to that point, my day had gone rather smoothly. I'm a real planner and had my whole day scheduled, down to the minute. What I didn't count on was five gallons of gas getting dumped into my vehicle. I mean, my parents' vehicle. I'll tell you what: that'll put a crimp in your plans! In a moment, my focus switched from my carefully laid-out agenda to scampering here and there, frantically calling this professional and that professional, trying to figure out what to do.

I didn't panic, though. In the midst of this formidable experience, I stopped, took a few deep breaths, and counted to one hundred. Soon, almost miraculously, I realized there was really nothing I could do about the situation. So I chose not to let it get me down. After that, I lightened up and smoothly moved through the rest of my day. Yeah, right! If you believe that, then I have some swamp land in South Florida I'd like to sell you.

What really happened: After talking to several professionals, I realized how much damage my blunder had actually caused and what a big hassle it was going to be to get it fixed. My stress level shot up to the top of the scale. I took deep breaths, all right, but they were breaths of frustration and self-aggravation. How could I have been so stupid? Hadn't I made extra sure the gas can was secured after I filled it up at the station? I just know I did. Didn't I?

After reaching almost total mental exhaustion, I decided simply not to deal with it anymore. So I opened all the windows to let the van air out and thought I would go ahead and cut the grass. Working in the yard is a stress reducer for me, and it would give me time to think about what to do. But wouldn't you know it, the !@#* mower wouldn't start! I pulled and pulled, jiggled and adjusted, then resorted to kicking and yelling. My three-week-old mower wouldn't start! It was ninety-five degrees outside. I was sweating like a lobster. In the distance, the telephone rang. I made a mad dash to answer it. It was my dad. I'm forty, and suddenly found myself on the receiving end of a lecture, as if I were ten, on how he never spilled gasoline, not once, in his entire life! My stress level then blew off the scale, and I muttered some most unkind words back to him.

Somehow, on that day, life had lost its luster. I didn't feel Christian. I didn't feel close to God. I didn't feel like this motivational, inspirational author and speaker that I'm supposed to be. The spilled gasoline was merely the straw that broke the camel's back, if you know what I mean. I was tired. Tired of the fight. Tired of the hassle of life. I wanted to quit, give up, throw in the towel. A flight to the Caribbean under a false name appealed to me. I had to get away—escape. Yet, I knew I couldn't. I have debt. I have a fourteen-year-old daughter, a twelve-year-old deaf son, a nine-year-old daughter, and a loving wife. They needed me. Someone had to keep the wheels rolling. I must push through this, I told myself. So I forced myself to put one weary foot in front of the other and move on. Yet deep inside I wondered, How much more stress can I take?

Not only did I feel stressed; I also felt stupid, embarrassed, and unlovable. And when I don't like myself, I am no fun to be around. My wife and children can attest to that. They, the ones closest to me, the ones I love the most, became the outlets for my frustration that day. As I did to my dad, I said things to them that stung, that wounded, words I didn't mean. The very instant these harsh utterances shot from my mouth, I wished I had them back. But too late. They were out, and the damage was done. Those venomous darts had stuck. And before my very eyes, I could see the poison starting to take its effect on them. My actions had been anything but Christian.

Suddenly, I found myself alone. It wasn't my choice. Nobody really wanted to be around me. I'd become one of those difficult people I counsel other people to protect themselves from. In my aloneness, I was all too aware of my low-life actions. With depression and exhaustion, I crashed on my bed. Then came guilt, massive waves of guilt. I could have tried to dismiss my feelings. I could have somehow justified my actions. But the fact is, this was not a case of "false" guilt as in Job's case. I was guilty. I ruined my parents' van. It was my responsibility. An accident, yes. However, I still owned my actions. Truthfully though, the accident was not what I felt guilty about. I felt stupid about it and my pocketbook stung because of it, but it had been my decision to react to my circumstances in a way that hurt those around me—for that, I was indeed guilty.

Now, I must tell you. Writing about myself, in such a light, is not easy. Exposing one's flaws never is. Allowing you to see this side of me puts my image as a helper of others at risk. It would be much easier to write nice, cheery words that make you feel good about me. But hey, from time to time, this is where I live, and I have an idea that, from time to time, you live there too.

Whenever I have one of these "moments of insanity," as I call them, there are several helpful things I can do to clear my mind and get to thinking rationally again. Exercise is one of them. It's amazing how our minds calm down when we exert our physical bodies. Exercise helps cleanse our systems of a toxic chemical called noradrenaline that builds up in our bodies when we are under stress. Along with adrenaline, noradrenaline is a hormone triggered into action by your brain when you become anxious.

The problem is, if you stay stressed, the brain continues to trigger more and more noradrenaline, leading to rage and other physical complications. Seventy-five percent of illnesses that result in a visit to the doctor's office are stress related.[29] Some signs of negative stress include rapid pulse, tense muscles, clenched jaw, shortness of breath, fear, panic, anxiety, irritability, or frequent anger. Wow! That was my day to a tee. I was experiencing all of the above.

Exercise is important because it induces relaxation by flooding your body with endorphins. Endorphins are natural sedatives released by the brain and other organs. Time and time again, after rigorous exercise, my perspective on life has changed. Things become more balanced. This is just one of the many reasons why exercise should be a part of our regular routine. Working in my yard and writing have also proven therapeutic for me. For you, there may be some other stress-relieving activity you enjoy doing.

In addition to exercise and therapeutic activities, some common stress-management techniques include deep breathing, meditation, stretching, and biofeedback. All these types of activities are helpful. They are important. We need to incorporate them into our daily routines. However, they can only offer help to a certain level. They deal primarily with the physical aspects of stress, but they don't help with the most powerful cause of stress on the soul—unresolved guilt.

Let's Talk About Guilt

Guilt is one of the most misunderstood emotions. There are both "true" guilt and "false" guilt, and regardless of which guilt we are carrying, it is vital that we get rid of it. Unresolved guilt, in whatever form, compounds our stress levels and destroys the soul. Many people are walking around with layers of compounded guilt weighing them down like a lead suit, and most of the time they don't even realize they are carrying it. Their guilt is so ingrained that it has become a part of their personality.

Donnie's story is a perfect example of "false" guilt. When Donnie was a child, his father and mother divorced. They constantly fought over child support and visitation rights, and several extended court battles ensued. One night, Donnie overheard his father say, in a fit of anger, "Paying child support is keeping me poor, and Donnie's birth was a stupid accident!" It's hard to imagine a parent feeling that way, yet scenes like this are repeated all across the United States. As a result, Donnie took on a deep-seated sense of "false" guilt and shame. He felt responsible for his parents' divorce and for their poor financial state. Before reaching his twentieth birthday, Donnie had made two attempts at suicide. Thankfully, he was unsuccessful and has since received help.

No doubt, "false" guilt and shame destroy. What I want to focus on now, though, is "true" guilt. Is there such a thing? Yes, and it is important, too, not that "true" guilt plays a critical role in healthy living. "True" guilt is not a negative emotion. Sharon Faelten and David Diamond, the editors of *Prevention* magazine, said in their book *Take Control of Your Life,* "For a while it was in vogue among pop psychologists to dub guilt as the 'useless' emotion and to attempt to banish it and its many stressful side effects from the psyche. But recently, therapists have been working to restore guilt to its rightful place among our emotions."[30] Charles Swindol said it best in his book *Stress Fractures,* so I'll let you read his words:

> Let's imagine a weird scene. Let's say that as two men are driving along, one of the lights on the dashboard starts flashing red. The driver says to his friend, "Hand me that hammer in the glove compartment, okay? Thanks." Tap . . . Tap . . . Bamm . . . Bamm ! . . Pow! "There! Now we've gotten rid of that light." Smoke is coming out of the hood, yet the guy keeps driving along.
>
> How foolish! And yet, it isn't difficult to find people who will hand out hammers. As they do, they say, Aw, that's needless guilt. . . . But wait . . . that's NECESSARY guilt! God help us when we don't have it! It's the conscience that bites into us

deep within and stings us when we compromise our moral purity . . . That's the red light flashing down inside. It's God's way of saying, "Pull over . . . stop. Lift the hood. Deal with the real problem."[31]

Willard Gaylin, M.D., author of *Feelings: Our Vital Signs,* says, "The sense of guilt you feel is what makes you human. Be grateful you have it."[32] Rabbi Harold Kushner said, "The purpose of guilt is to make us feel bad for the right reasons." A part of being human is the ability to experience "true" guilt. The point of experiencing "true" guilt is not so we can say, "Hey, I'm guilty," and then move on with life, but so we can deal with our guilt, make the needed adjustments, and have it lifted from us. We don't have to live with guilt, even if we are guilty.

I realize that I'm stepping out on a huge limb with my next point. Many New Agers and self-help teachers will take issue with what I'm about to say; however, understanding this truth is fundamental to experiencing the freedom and joy that go beyond description, even in the midst of trying circumstances. Simply put, *the human race is guilty.* The Old Testament Jewish prophet Isaiah said, *"We all, like sheep, have gone astray."*[33] I'm guilty. You're guilty. We're all guilty. Every single person who has ever lived, save one, has fallen short. I don't know about you, but that brings me great comfort. And any person who looks honestly within himself and says that he's never fallen short or blown it is in serious denial or ignorance. Mother Teresa once said, "It is easy to be proud and harsh and selfish—so easy. But we have been created for better things. Each of us has plenty of good as well as plenty of bad in us . . ."[34] Even Mother Teresa admits to having some bad in her.

The answer to our guilt is not to hammer it out, to say we're not guilty when we are and simply gloss over our blunders and, yes, our sins.

God has given you a free will, and you have the power to choose. If you choose the hammering-out method, your heart will become calloused, and as time passes, little by little, you'll get what you want: less feeling of guilt. But I ask, "Is that what you really want?" The guilt will still be there. But you won't feel it. Or you may feel it, in the form of high blood pressure or irritability, or worse yet, in being out of fellowship with God. One doesn't have to be a murderer or a thief to be guilty and have a calloused heart. There are many "nice" people who are hardened deep within.

But this hardening of the heart is not what God intended. It's not God's best. God wants you to experience freedom and transformation. Don't let someone or some guru give you a mere hammer to whack out God's voice in your life. Listen to your heart.

There's only one thing I've found that can neutralize "true" guilt and give us the lasting freedom that most of us are longing for. It's grace—God's grace. Again, I'm going to make a statement that goes against the grain of what many self-help gurus teach, and even what some preachers preach. Nevertheless, it, too, is the truth. I use the word *truth* with great conviction. At first, your emotions may scream otherwise, but deep down in the alcoves of your soul, you'll know it's the truth. Here it is. Grab hold of this and don't let it go: *We can't do it. We can't do life. We can't even do the Christian life, or the Jewish life, or whatever. And the more we try to change ourselves through our own willpower, the more frustrated we will become. You and I need grace in order to do life. We need lots and lots of grace. And the good news is: Grace is what God is all about.*

Am I saying that we are doomed to be controlled by our unwanted self-defeating behaviors? That we can't change? That it's okay to justify being a jerk to our loved ones as I had been the day I spilled the gasoline? Not at all. What I'm saying is that God can and will transform us into totally new creatures, but it won't happen through our own willpower, and we will never be sinlessly perfect. Here lies the great mystery to personal freedom: *God's grace is what changes us.* God's power for living comes through acknowledging our personal weakness. Coming to a point of weakness is one of the most powerful spiritual places one can be.

Some people think they can do life on their own. So they grit their teeth and muster all their human powers. They set out with great energy and resolve to be all they can be. This works for a little while, until failure strikes again and again. It's only when our human efforts are exhausted that God comes to us with a comforting message—the message of Grace.

A Warm Picture of God's Grace

One Sunday afternoon, my wife, Alanna, and I were driving through our neighborhood when we saw the cutest little blond-headed boy at the street's edge holding up a cardboard poster that read KOOL-AID 25 CENTS. The weather was hot, really hot, Louisiana hot. The boy was five, maybe six, and his older, much wiser sister (maybe nine) tended the money and drinks some thirty feet back off the street. Business was slow, and both Alanna and I could see the desperation in the little boy's face. As we slowed down, Alanna fumbled in her purse for fifty cents. An expression of surprise swept across the boy's face, as if to say, "Hey, we have a customer, an actual customer!" Then he paused, almost frozen, unsure of what to do next. Slowly, he inched his way to the car window. At that moment, his expression changed and seemed to say "Are you sure? Do you really want to buy Kool-Aid from me, a little kid?"

Still unsure, he glanced back at his sister. She waved at him: "Go ahead." Alanna placed two shiny quarters in his hand. For a few brief seconds, he just stood and stared at his hand. Then reality hit: "Two quarters!" He turned and dashed to the stand with excitement. Shortly afterward, he came creeping back, cautiously, so as not to spill a single drop, with two extremely small bathroom dispenser cups full of green Kool-Aid. My wife and I took them and offered our words of encouragement. As we drove off, Alanna peered down at hers, giggled, then looked at me, and said, "I'm not drinking mine." I was more daring. I took a sip—almost pure sugar water with one piece of melting ice. "I'm not either," I responded. As soon as we were out of the children's view, we poured the Kool-Aid out and looked at each other with big smiles.

What a picture of God's grace! Most of us, deep in

our hearts, want to please God with our lives. We desire to make a difference. So often, though, our best efforts get watered down in the heat of stressful circumstances and we are overwhelmed by our guilt. When this happens, our temptation is to give up and believe that we have nothing God wants.

Yet, just as Alanna and I did with those kids, God does with us. He takes the initiative. He's stopping by our lives and saying, "Give me what you've got." He's not asking you to clean up your act and get perfect before you come to Him. Your best efforts may be weak and watered down, with loads of unwanted sugar, but God wants to take it. Does God need our Kool-Aid? I don't think so. God doesn't need our watered-down efforts and mistakes. He needs us. Remember that God loved us first. That's why He's trying to give us two quarters for whatever we have. Not because we deserve it, or because what we're offering is worth His price. We could never pay the price that God paid for us.

I love the passage of Scripture found in Psalm 103:8–14. It has become a pillar in my life. Maybe it can become a pillar in yours, too. Read it slowly and let it sink into your inner being.

The Lord is compassionate and gracious, slow to anger, abounding in love. . . . He does not treat us as our sins deserve or repay us according to our iniquities. For as high as the heavens are above the earth, so great is his love for those who fear him. . . . As a father has compassion on his children, so the Lord has compassion on

*those who fear him; for he knows how we are formed,
he remembers that we are but dust.*

Look at God's attributes! God is compassionate, slow
to anger, abounding in love! And it gets better. He does
not treat us as our sins deserve. Thank God, or I'd be in
big trouble! Oh, how I love the last line of this passage,
". . . for he knows how we are formed, he remembers
that we are but dust."

Did you get that? God remembers that we are but
mere imperfect humans. He knows perfectly well that
we are not divine like Him, nor does He expect us to be.
That's why He's made provision for us. God knows all
about us. He knows who we are, and what we are. God
knows we are but children on a street corner offering up
the best we have. Quite often, the storms we are experiencing in life are a direct result of our own blunders and
sins. Sometimes our lives get watered down in the heat of
stress. Yet, God chooses to stop and take part in our lives
anyway. We, on the other hand, like the little boy, act
surprised when God says, "Here are two quarters of
Grace." All we have to do is take them. When we do,
God smiles.

What I'm learning to do, personally, is to refrain
from fighting and struggling and determine to be a better person. Instead, I admit my inadequacies and, in
humility, offer them up to God. When I do this, something truly supernatural takes place. Grace takes place.
God fills me with His overwhelming peace and forgiveness. Joy floods my soul. A desire is created in me not to

repeat my actions. Yes, there are consequences to my actions. Sin hurts people and ourselves. That is why God hates it so much. Yet experiencing God's grace gives power, and as time passes, by God's spirit in me, not my mere human efforts, I begin to change.

The key to the secret of Grace is not working hard to be a great person, putting forth an image of being a person who has it all together, but being real and working at turning our shortcomings over to God.

After I received forgiveness from God for my "moment of insanity" with the gasoline and after I forgave myself, I then went to my wife, to each of my children, and to my dad and asked them to forgive me also. They were ready and willing. It's amazing the response we get when we simply admit to the ones we've offended that we blew it.

5.

Nourishing
the Soul

Soulfulness . . . Its goal is not to make life problem-free, but to give ordinary life depth and value.

—THOMAS MOORE, *CARE OF THE SOUL*

In 1871 it all came crashing down. Everything—a total loss. Years of investing, planning, and hard work, gone in an instant, in a puff of smoke—literally. Attorney Horatio Spafford had amassed a great fortune from investing heavily in real estate on the shores of Lake Michigan. But the great Chicago fire of 1871 wiped out his entire holding, leaving him deeply in debt and on the verge of bankruptcy.

It was such a stressful time for the family that Mrs. Spafford's health began to fail. By 1873, her health had declined so much that her physician advised her to take a trip to ease the stress. Horatio, Mrs. Spafford, and their four daughters planned a long family vacation to Europe, but an abrupt business concern forced Horatio to delay his departure. His wife and four daughters sailed as intended on the ship *Ville du Havre*. Horatio planned to catch up with them in Europe a short time later, but that never happened. In the late-night darkness, on rough stormy seas, the *Ville du Havre* ran head-on into another ship and sank. Amid churning waves and high winds, Mrs. Spafford watched in horror as her four daughters were swept away to their deaths.

As she was fighting for her last breath, a falling mast knocked her unconscious. Amazingly, Mrs. Spafford's body snagged on a floating piece of wreckage, and she later revived. She and a few others were rescued. From Europe, she cabled two words to Horatio: "Saved Alone."

Horatio immediately set sail to meet his wife in Cardiff, Wales. He requested that the ship take the same route that his family's ship had taken. All the way, his heart ached, and he cried out to God in deep pain. As the ship neared the site of the tragedy, Horatio asked the captain to stop. He leaned over the ship's railing and gazed down at the spot where his daughters' lives were lost and began to pray. It was there that Horatio Spafford was overwhelmed by a great peace. While enveloped in this peace, he penned the following words:

> *When peace like a river attendeth my way,*
> *When sorrows like sea-bellows roll,*
> *Whatever my lot, Thou hast taught me to say:*
> *It is well, it is well with my soul.*

But Lord, 'tis for thee, for thy coming we wait,
The sky, not the grave, is our goal;
O trump of the angel! O voice of the Lord!
Blessed hope, blessed rest of my soul![35]

These words were turned into a hymn, which through the decades has been a source of inspiration for untold millions.

How could a man who had lost all his investments, and then four daughters, possibly write such words? It seems impossible. How could he experience such a peace when so many others in equally desperate situations do not? If you recall, during the Great Depression of the 1920s and '30s, many of those committed suicide. A man in my community just committed suicide after his wife left him. They had two small children. But instead of being suicidal, Horatio Spafford experienced *peace like a river*. How could that be?

Could it be that Horatio Spafford's soul was nourished and centered on God—on whom he had laid a foundation so that he had something to draw upon in his time of need? My godly grandmother once told me, "Trials don't make you who you are; they reveal who you are." That's a powerful statement. I'm sure Horatio experienced all the pain, grief, and questions that go along with deep personal trauma. Yet, in the midst of such a storm, Horatio was kept safe by God's supernatural peace because what was deep inside of his soul swelled up to the surface in his time of need. Within his being lay a reservoir of power that he could tap.

Proverbs 4:23 declares, *"Above all else, guard your*

heart (soul), for it is the wellspring of life." When I was young, I loved to visit my grandmother's house. She lived in a small country town, and right in the middle of town was a natural wellspring. Pure, sparkling, refreshing water bubbled up endlessly from deep below the ground. Each time we visited, my dad would bring two or three empty milk jugs and we would go down to the wellspring and fill them up. Today, that same wellspring is the source of a bottled water company that ships natural spring water all over the United States.

Your soul is also a natural wellspring. Whatever is in that well bubbles up and out, affecting your life. If your soul is nourished, your life will be full of the fruits of that nourishment. But if your soul is malnourished, your life will reflect a malnourished soul. That's why Proverbs says, *"Above all else,"* first, before anything, *"guard your soul!"* Take care of your soul. Protect your soul. Feed your soul. Nourish your soul! Nourishing the soul is beneficial not only for the sweet by-and-by, but also for the difficult now-and-now. If the soul is nourished, we will be centered on God and find power and strength in times of need. There is no peace that exists on Earth like the peace that comes when the soul is properly nourished and centered on God, and one is living and moving out of that center. It requires faith and choice, but nourishing our soul is the single most important thing we can do for ourselves and for those who are part of our daily lives.

It is important to note that when we focus on nourishing our soul, we are not being selfish. It is only through a nourished soul that we can become an oasis of nourishment for others. What bubbles up from within our soul spills over to those around us. And because what is bubbling out of us is natural and not manufactured, people are drawn to us. When our soul is nourished, we don't have to try to be anything or prove what we are. We just are what we are. We stop trying to give something that we don't have.

Our life ceases to be defined by tons of overextending activities (religious or not) that we feel we "should do" to feel right with God. Instead, we know God personally—not just about Him. He's with us every day, everywhere. Thus, the supermarket becomes as sacred as the chapel. We may still participate in organized religious traditions, probably more than ever, but they take on new meaning. We're not doing them out of a sense of obligation, but rather out of thanksgiving. Like a beautiful rose, we neither toil nor strain, yet we grow, even through painful circumstances, into what God desires us to be. This nourishing is a lifetime process.

Whoever you may be, regardless of your station in life, *now* is the time to begin your journey of the soul. You're never too young or too old to begin. This journey will take you on amazing adventures you can't begin to imagine. And it will give you a foundation that will withstand the storms of life blowing against you. If you are to live, I mean truly live, you must not put it off. God has a unique plan for you that begins with Himself. Don't delay. Life is fleeting.

To my Christian family, I must point out that Christ,

himself, said, *"I have come that you may have* life *and have it more* abundantly" (John 10:10). I ask you, "Are you truly experiencing that abundant life, or are you merely going through religious motions? Is Christ your best friend?"

To my Jewish friends, I wish to point out what the Psalmist wrote so eloquently in Psalm 40:2, 3, *"The Lord . . . lifted me out of the slimy pit, out of the mud and mire; He set my feet on a rock and gave me a firm place to stand. He put a new song in my mouth . . ."* God desires to lift us out of our slimy pits and muddy ruts and put a new song in our mouths! What song is that? It's the song that comes from having a nourished soul and being centered on God. I also make this plea to those of all other faiths and to those of no faith. Your life can be a master painting, a harmonized symphony that will bring nourishment to you, while also bringing nourishment to others.

I have a friend who is a devout atheist. We have a wonderful friendship because we are honest with each other. On numerous occasions, I've said to him, "Hey, if I'm wrong, I haven't missed out on anything. My life is filled with incredible joy and fulfillment. God has shown Himself to be real to me." Then I add, "But if you're wrong, you've lost everything!" Are you ready to take the risk of faith, even in the midst of all your questions, fears, and yes, pain? Despite all that, you can experience the fruits of soul nourishment. But you must make the choice to begin the journey. When you do, I guarantee that God will meet you there. What do you have to lose?

Beginning the Journey

To nourish our souls and become centered with God, we must first have a paradigm shift in our thinking. It is vital that we uncover what *kills* the soul and refocus our lives on what's really important.

Three Soul Killers

Soul Killer #1: Too Much Diversion

In his remarkable book *Tyranny of the Urgent,* Charles Hummel surmises that we habitually let the *urgent* things in our lives take priority over the *important* things in our lives. I believe one of the greatest tragedies of our modern society is the tragedy of diversion. We've become so busy running to and fro, doing this and that, trying to beat the system, that we are constantly diverted from the most important things in our lives, beginning with our very soul.

Technology has helped create more leisure time for the average person. Even so, few of us complain about having too much time to spare. There's always something or someone trying to divert us from simply slowing down and getting to know ourselves, our families, and God. We have the automobiles and airplanes to enhance travel; now we simply travel farther and faster. The fax and e-mail have made reports- and letters-on-demand the norm. We have ATMs, fast-food restaurants, microwaves, cell phones, and the Internet, but we have very little downtime. The economy is flourishing, but while having money is a nice thing, it's certainly not the answer. Statistics show that the more money people make, the more debt and pressure they have.

But we can't blame all our diversions on society or others. A large portion of the problem involves ourselves. As long as we convince ourselves that we are too busy and we keep putting ourselves in a position to be loaded down with more work and responsibility, we don't have to look at ourselves honestly and address personal issues. It's often easier to be busy. When we finally do slow down physically, so often, our minds are still racing.

Making the choice to slow down and quiet the mind requires the self-discipline and confidence to say "no" to the demands of others and to overcommitting yourself, and "yes" to simplifying your life. It may be hard at first and you may even feel guilty, but soon you will find that this is the right thing to do. As you learn to say "no," you're going to begin to have more time on your hands. This is the first step to a nourished soul. As Elaine St. James says in *Living the Simple Life,* "An amazing thing happens when we slow down. We start to get flashes of inspiration. We reach a new level of understanding and even wisdom. In a quiet moment we can get an intuitive insight that can change our entire life and the lives of the people around us."[36] To begin to nourish our souls, we must first slow down and focus on what's really important.

Christ told a parable about a farmer who went out one day to plant seeds. Some of the seeds were trampled on and never had a chance to grow. Some of them took root and began to grow but were choked by thorns and weeds. The thorns and weeds represent the things in life that are constantly diverting and choking out the things of God, keeping us from nourishing our souls.[37] Too much diversion kills the soul.

Soul Killer #2: Too Much Amusement

On the heels of diversion has come the age of amusement and entertainment. Past generations lived in a survival mode. They did not even know what leisure time was. My dad, for example, woke up every morning before daylight and milked cows. He then went to school. After school, he milked the cows again until suppertime. On Saturday, he worked again. Finally, on Saturday night he got to go out with his friends, and on Sunday, the whole family rested, like most of society at that time. Life was simpler, but in many ways harder.

Today, we technically have more leisure time, but it seems we have less quality time. We generally fill our spare time with an abundance of soul-killing amusements. The word we use for amusement was handed down from the ancient Greeks and actually means to "suspend the mind" or "not to think." When a person is being entertained or amused, he or she doesn't have to think. The mind is in neutral.

Certainly, there is a place for amusement. There are times when the mind needs a break and needs to be entertained. But that's not the problem for us. The problem is, simply put, we don't know how to be quiet and alone. We're afraid of silence. We are afraid of boredom.

If used properly, times of boredom can be offered up

to God and become some of life's most rewarding experiences, unleashing our creativity. But nowadays, the moment we find ourselves bored, it's so easy to pop in a video or engage in other activities that rob us of precious time that could be used for nourishing our soul. Just as we have a hard time saying no to people and commitments, so we have a hard time saying no to amusement. When we are being amused, our creative mind is generally suspended.

Imagine for a moment that, one day, a rich uncle hands you a check, made out to you, in the amount of $86,400. Your eyes bug out and your jaw hits the ground. You can't believe your good fortune. Then, just before you're about to give your uncle a great big bear hug, he says, "You have one day, exactly twenty-four hours, to invest as much of that money as possible. You can invest it any way you wish, in any project you wish, but at the end of the time period, any money that's not invested, I get back."[38] What do you think the average person would do if he or she had an opportunity like this? I know what I would do. I'd have my mind and body in gear trying to invest as much money as possible. I wouldn't want to lose one red cent. Call it a hunch, but I think that's what most people would do, too.

Well, did you know that every day, each of us is given 86,400 seconds of time? We are free to invest those seconds any way we choose, but at the end of the day, they are gone—never to return. You never get another chance to live today again. On top of that, there is no guarantee that we will have another tomorrow. How are you investing your seconds? Are you throwing away precious time on wasteful activities, or are you investing it in ways that nourish your soul?

The most common excuse most people make for their lack of devotion to renewal and personal-growth activities is their lack of time. Let's get real, folks. The average American watches thirty to forty hours of television a week! We're all busy people, but still, for most of us, it's not a matter of time, but a matter of priorities. I find that the most successful and fulfilled people I meet are extremely busy, yet they know how to use their time wisely. Most have developed strong time-management skills.

In all fairness, I do realize that there is truth in statements such as "An idle mind is the devil's workshop." We need focus. Our children need focus. And please don't misunderstand me: I'm not against having fun. The challenge is to fill our time with activities that nourish the soul and release our spirit instead of activities that kill the soul and fill our minds with garbage.

When our minds are amused and in this state of suspension, we allow all types of soul-killing ideas to influence our intellect. And we spend precious little time in spiritual renewal. When I say spiritual renewal, I don't mean sitting in a room somewhere with your legs crossed and your palms in the air saying *"Ammmmmmm."* You could take a walk or go for a jog. I like mountain biking. I tell you what, my soul opens up when I'm on the bike trail; my soul opens up when I work in the yard.

The point is, it's vital that you find a way to connect with God. And yes, sometimes it will require the discipline of saying "no" to amusement and getting quiet so you can hear that still, small voice that's wanting to communicate. Too much amusement kills the soul.

Soul Killer #3: Too Much Stuff

Stuff clutters. Stuff complicates. Stuff restricts. Stuff hinders. There are multitudes of people who can't do what their soul is calling them to do because they have too much stuff. Stuff requires responsibility. One of the key words that frees the soul is *less*. When a rich, young ruler came to Jesus, his soul was crying out to follow Him. Jesus told him to go sell all his possessions and give them to the poor, and then he could follow Him. The young man hung his head and walked away, saddened. He couldn't let go of all his stuff. His stuff was keeping him from experiencing an incredible journey of the soul with Christ. I don't know for certain, but I imagine when the man went back home to all his stuff, it suddenly seemed very unfulfilling.[39]

Something I've discovered is that stuff can't fulfill. It leaves an empty spot in the soul. If you are pursuing a dream or a vocation just to get stuff, in the end you may have a beautiful house set on a hill, but you'll have a soul in the gutter. It seems, year after year, we hear of yet more rich and famous people committing suicide or having drug problems, etc. Why? Because after a lifetime of pursuing fame and having all the things money could buy, they were still empty. They discovered, the hard way, that stuff can't fulfill.

At his death, billionaire Howard Hughes left a legacy of two billion dollars. Yet he spent the last ten years of his life as a recluse. When he died, he left no wife or children to mourn for him. Even with all his wealth, his life and death produced great loneliness.

Billionaire John Paul Getty had accumulated from two to four billion dollars in the oil business. But his private life was in shambles. He had married and divorced five times. His youngest son died of pneumonia in 1953, and in 1973 his eldest son died an alcoholic.

If the abundance of material possessions brought happiness, these two billionaires should have had the greatest happiness of all.

Listen carefully to what I am *not* saying. I'm not saying the answer is to go sell everything you have. Jesus wasn't saying that, either. Jesus knew that stuff was the real God. That's why He asked the rich young ruler to sell everything. Jesus wanted to see which God the man would serve.

Having stuff is not bad. But the pursuit of stuff, for stuff's sake, kills the soul. To follow your soul's calling, you may have to do without some things, but you will experience such joy and fulfillment that you won't even miss them. Chances are, if you pursue your soul's calling, you'll eventually be in a place to have nice things and really enjoy them because you'll have them, they won't have you. St. Paul said, " I have learned to be content whether I have a lot or a little."[40] What Paul was saying was that his happiness didn't have to do with his stuff but with his soulfulness.

An acquaintance of mine is a doctor. He was once the extremely successful head of a thriving medical clinic. He loved his work, he had a $600,000 home, a beautiful wife, and three children. Yet, his soul wasn't fulfilled. He felt God was calling him to start an inner-city clinic for the underprivileged. As time passed, the gnawing inside his soul got greater and greater until he couldn't take it anymore. Starting the new clinic would require him to cut back his hours drastically, which would mean less money. It would also mean a sizable financial investment. All of this spelled R-I-S-K.

Still, he took the idea before his family, told them what he felt God was calling him to do, and laid out the plan. He told them this was his heart's desire, but he wouldn't do it unless they were all in agreement. He let them know that they would still be provided for, but the family would have to make some serious cutbacks. The first thing they would have to do is downsize and simplify, which meant selling their expensive home in a country club. After several days of thinking it over, his family agreed to the plan.

I salute this family. They didn't let the love of stuff keep them from God's best. To fulfill your soul's calling, you may have to change some things. You might have to downsize to get started. You *will* have to take a risk. And if you are holding on to stuff, it won't happen. Too much stuff kills the soul.

Three Soul Nourishers

1. Feeding on Soul Food

Each of us has the ability to choose whether we will be a victim in life or a problem solver. The way we choose to respond to our circumstances is completely up to us. Personal responsibility does not necessarily mean taking the blame for something; it also means the ability to respond—response-ability.

Choice is what makes us uniquely human and separates us from the animals. God doesn't want robots. He wants a creation that will respond to Him. There can be no love without choice. This is one reason God doesn't just reveal Himself openly. God stays somewhat hidden, because He wants us to seek Him—to find Him. He leaves clues all around, evidence of His majesty. As we pick up one clue after another, God reveals a little more of Himself. But each step requires the choice of faith. As time passes, our faith grows. Without faith, it is impossible to find God. God wants us to search for Him, to know Him as He knows us.

In biblical times, when Jesus spoke, He usually spoke in parables. For years, I thought He did so in order to illuminate a point. However, this was not the case at all. According to Scripture and most biblical scholars, Jesus spoke in parables to *conceal* a point and require the listener to search for it. Those who chose faith and searched would find a pearl of great wisdom. But those who chose not to believe would walk away cynical and confused. Jesus was trying to draw faith out of His hearers.

Choice is one of *the* most powerful gifts God has bestowed on humanity. Nourishing our soul and becoming centered on God begin with choice. And *choice always begins in the mind,* not the emotions. The mind is the seat of the soul. This is why the first step in feeding our soul begins in the mind—we choose with the mind to feed on good things.

Look at a clock with a second hand. Now, watch thirty seconds tick by. It's not a long time, is it? Yet, large corporations pay millions of dollars to advertise their thirty-second commercials. Why? How can they justify spending that kind of money for such short spots? It's because advertisers know that what we, as consumers, put before our eyes really does influence us. Rarely will a company run only one advertisement. Instead, the same spot will run over and over and over again. Eventually, the repetition plants into our minds the message the advertiser is trying to get across. How many times have you caught yourself singing some silly commercial jingle as you went about your daily business? Or better yet, how many times have you used the word *Coke* when you meant "soft drink"? Or *Kleenex* when you meant "tissue"? What we put before our eyes and in our minds does affect us.

A comedian once said, "If you eat fat and greasy food, you become a fat and greasy dude!" It's true. You are what you eat. For many of us, our soul is malnourished because we feed on a diet of junk food and negative input. We seldom, if ever, take time to cleanse ourselves and put into our soul a healthy diet.

But just as a physical transformation takes place when we change our eating and exercise patterns, our souls are transformed when we change what we feed it. Romans 12:2 says, *"Do not conform any longer to the pattern of this world, but be transformed by the renewing of your mind."* I don't understand how it happens, but a supernatural transformation takes place when we renew our minds. Neither do I understand how a tiny seed, when it is planted in the ground, grows into a mighty tree. God has miraculously placed life into it. Everyone has within his soul a seed of faith—a measure of faith. The potential is there in all of us to grow a beautiful garden of wonderful fruit. It's part of being created in God's image. Yet, if that seed is to grow and produce fruit, it must be fed and tended. Conforming to the world system takes no effort. Anyone can conform. You just let life and the system take you where they take you, and you merely hang on for the ride. It's like a garden. If you just let it go, there will be weeds everywhere. Nothing will make sense.

Feeding on soul food, on the other hand, takes time. It takes a choice. We have to unplug from the world system and plug into the power source. Like a caring gardener, we must tend to our garden. We are in partnership with God. Only God can cause the transformation and growth to take place, but we must do the tending and watering.

Once upon a time, a country preacher bought an overgrown piece of land. There were vines everywhere, almost covering the trees. The thorns and thistles were so thick the preacher could hardly walk. But each weekend, he worked his land—cutting away all the unwanted excess, burning it, breaking up the ground, planting seeds, fertilizing, watering, and then tending the soil by keeping the weeds out. Days turned into weeks. Weeks turned into months. Soon, the farmer's garden began to produce a beautiful harvest. One day, a friend stopped by and said, "Preacher, God sure has blessed you with a fruitful piece of land." To that, the preacher replied, "Yes He has, but you should have seen it when God had it all to Himself!"

Feeding the soul and becoming centered on God take time. It takes cultivation. After a time, what you feed on becomes a part of your personality. You become more influenced by positive than negative truth. This allows you to respond differently in trying situations. Feeding doesn't make you right with God; it opens you up to God. It's not a chore; rather, it becomes a part of what you are. Feeding on soul food is so important because it brings everything in your life into perspective.

A balanced soul-food diet consists of the following:

- Simplifying life so you can free up time to feed your soul

- Meditating daily on Scripture

- Applying action to Scripture

- Reading good, uplifting literature that stretches the mind

- Consistent prayer (talking honestly with God)

- Blocking out distractions so you can hear that still, small voice inside of you

- Pondering inspired works of art and listening to inspired music

- Gleaning insight from the stories and teachings of others

- Spending time outside in nature (When God created man, He placed him in a garden. Being in nature opens the soul.)

- Exercising and eating healthy foods. When our body is sharp, our minds are sharp.

2. Heeding the Moment

The most important moment of your life is the moment you are experiencing right now. Don't miss it by living in the past or in the future. Many people are so busy dealing with their past that they can't see the now. Others are so focused on future events that they miss the blessings at hand. The soul becomes full when we slow down and absorb all the little moments throughout the day. It's in these small fragments of time that God illuminates truth to our soul. We can't do without our soul-feeding times, but living in the now, giving heed to the priceless small moments throughout the day, waters the seeds we have planted during our soul feedings.

One night not long ago, I was dropping two children off at their home after they had spent the weekend with our family. They live about two hours from my house, and their parents were aware that I would be bringing them home about eleven. I live on seventy acres, which is considered to be in the country, but this family lives in the "country country." The closest town to their house has only five thousand people, and it is twenty minutes away from them.

At the entrance to their gravel driveway is a closed cattle gate. As I stopped the car, one of the children hopped out to open it, only to discover that the gate was locked. At first I didn't think much about it, then the children informed me that it was almost a mile from the gate to the house. Get this picture: it's eleven o'clock at night, it's chilly, the gravel road to the house meanders through a pasture and woods. You can't even see the house from the road. We're out in the middle of nowhere. I have a two-hour drive back home. The nearest gas station is fifteen miles down the road, and I don't have my cell phone. I started to feel my anger boiling up a bit. "Those idiots," I thought to myself. "How could they not unlock the gate? They knew we were coming." The children started murmuring as well. Then, an inspired thought hit me. "Don't blow this moment. God has something in mind for the now."

With that, I told the children to get their things, that we were going on a hike. At first they were a little scared, yet as we walked, the stars shone brightly and we had the most awesome experience. The whole way, we talked about the stars and God, and before you knew it, we were at the house. The parents were sitting in their living room watching television. They were very apologetic—they thought the kids knew the combination to the gate's lock. They offered to give me a ride back to my car. But I was having such an inspired moment that I said, "You know, I'd rather walk." On the way back, I had the most wonderful talk with God. I'm so glad I opened up to the moment instead of opening up to anger, frustration, and haste. Sure, I got home a little bit later, but I know in my soul, God gave me that moment.

Living in the moment brings inspiration to our souls. When you are fully present in the now—when you are focusing on what lies directly before you—you will experience a completeness in every experience you have, and your soul will be nourished.

3. Seeding into Others

Have you ever wondered how Mother Teresa could live in the world's most impoverished city, Calcutta, completely surrounded by diseased, malnourished, and dying people and yet be so at peace and fulfilled? Do you think she ever missed living in a normal home, in a normal neighborhood, with a normal life? I don't think so. I believe Mother Teresa was so fulfilled in her soul that she never really thought about it. Her focus was on two primary things: a relationship with God and the needs of those around her. As she poured out what God had placed inside her, she received back supernatural strength and peace from God. That's the only way she could continue doing what she did year after year. A solid, life-transforming principle is: You can't out-give God. The more you seed into the lives of others, the more it will come back to you.

The story of Johan Eriksson is an extraordinary example of what it means to seed into the lives of others. During the Holocaust, trainloads of Jewish children were arriving daily in Sweden. Most of these children were malnourished, thin, and pale, with dark eyes sunken into their heads. They carried no belongings except identification tags around their necks and despondent expressions.

Many Swedish families agreed to take in children for the "duration of the war." One of the Swedes who offered his home was Johan Eriksson. When Johan learned of a nine-year-old boy named Rolf who needed a home, his heart went out with compassion. Since Johan was a devout Baptist, little Rolf had to adjust to the Baptist way of life. In the beginning, when knocks came at the door, the boy would dive under the covers or hide in a closet. Yet again and again, Johan would shower him with love and assurance. Soon, Rolf began to gain weight, and the despondent gaze left his eyes. Eventually, he began to laugh again.

When the threat of a Nazi invasion seemed certain, Johan's workmates would say, "When Hitler comes, you will be in trouble with that Jew boy in your house." Johan would tighten his jaw and clinch his fist and say, "They'll never take him so long as I'm alive."

In addition to the Nazi threat, Johan was getting pressure from his fellow Baptists. Members of the church assumed that Johan would try to convert the boy. When confronted, Johan's jaw would tighten again. The Swedish government had promised the Jewish refugee organization that the children's religion would be kept intact. Johan went to great lengths to see that Rolf's religious heritage was maintained. He took the boy to church with his family but saw to it that Rolf learned Jewish traditions so that when he reached the proper age, he was prepared for and celebrated his Bar Mitzvah. When the war was over, Johan wanted to return to Rolf's parents a son who had been raised as closely as possible in the way they would have wished. After the war, however, Rolf's parents were never found. They had died in concentration camps along with millions of others.

Rolf grew up. But the events of his past caught up with him, and he suffered a mental breakdown. Because he was thought to be dangerous, the authorities sought to put him in a mental institution. But Johan would not allow it. "He belongs here," Johan insisted. "This is his home." For over a year, Johan nursed Rolf back to mental stability and calmness. Rolf's life was relatively untroubled after that. Yet he never forgot the man who planted into his life the seeds of unconditional love.[41] Johan was never the same, either. Because he gave out of his soul, his soul became full.

Once you've cultivated your soul and it is producing fruit, that fruit may rot if it just sits. You have to begin to feed others and plant the seeds of your fruit in their lives. This is the final key to a nourished soul.

Having a nourished soul that is centered on God gives us power and peace from God to make it through the most trying experiences life can throw at us. It also enriches our day-to-day existence. Your soul is a wellspring of life. Now, go nourish it.

6.

From Disappointment to Reappointment

I am no longer afraid of becoming lost, because the journey back always reveals to me something new about my life and about my own humanity, and that is, ultimately, good for the artist.

—BILLY JOEL

If you met my friend Tessa you would, at once, be drawn to her warm personality, the high degree of intellectual stimulation she offers in conversation, and most of all, the authenticity of her spirit. She is a successful teacher of inner-city children, and when I first heard her story of triumph over disappointment and broken dreams, I knew I wanted to share it with others.

At age thirteen, Tessa's mother died, leaving a void in her life that made growing up much tougher than for most children. Fortunately, Tessa had a special aunt, who became a pillar in her life. Tessa spent many days and nights visiting her aunt's home. It was a place of love and warmth, filled with delightful aromas forever seeping out from the kitchen and infiltrating the entire house. Tessa's aunt was a stay-at-home mom and a masterful homemaker. When visiting, Tessa would gaze at her from a distance and dream of one day being a home-maker just like her, living in a warm and loving home just like hers. As Tessa grew up, this was her vision of how her life was going to be—of how her life *should* be. She was going to get married, have children, and build a wonderful family home.

Tessa did indeed get married to her "Prince Charming" and started building her dream house. All was well, until her husband became addicted to alcohol and drugs and she found out he was being unfaithful to her. After Tessa confronted him, he promised to change. Yet the chemical abuse and unfaithfulness continued. Tessa's dreams were shattered, and she found herself on her own, as a single mom with three children. To make matters worse, she had no career to fall back on because all her life she had prepared to be a homemaker. The breakup of her marriage hit Tessa hard. She fought continual bouts of overwhelming depression and fear and lost an unhealthy amount of weight. Life seemed hopeless. During this time, Tessa wrote a letter to herself that expressed her feelings:

> *Tonight, the girls and I decorated the Christmas tree. We spent the evening frolicking around the tree farm in search of that perfect tree with the most fluff. I sampled*

every one of them and was sure that we had picked the one that smelled the most like Christmas. Driving home was fun; the girls giggled as we passed cars on the street with our tree sticking two feet out of the trunk of the car. Now, after angel kisses and reprimands for feeding cheddar crackers to Gabby, the dog, they sleep peacefully. I sneaked upstairs to release the tears that I've held back all evening.

This is the second Christmas that the kids and I have spent alone without their daddy. This is the time of year for families, and my heart longs for us to be together. Although that longing is inside of me, I know that my health and my children's future depend upon my being strong. It's a tough fight, but giving in to that longing would just bring more unbearable pain and ultimate destruction. I've learned that doing what's right sometimes means standing alone, and I've found that being alone isn't nearly as painful as being lonely.

I was married fifteen years to a man who loved life but made wrong choices. I watched the man I loved grow more and more dependent upon alcohol to escape the stress of life, and I watched our lives disintegrate before my eyes. I tried for years to hold on to a dream that would never come true. I was like a squirrel gathering nuts and storing them inside a burning tree in the middle of a forest fire. I continued working to build a home for my family until I completely exhausted myself both mentally and physically.

Each time I would cry for help, my husband would make excuses; many times it was "my" fault. Then he would promise to end the cycle. But it never stopped.

The only way to stop the pain of abuse and the betrayal of infidelity was to stop waiting for him to get help and to make the decision to help my children and myself.

I continuously questioned if I was doing the right thing. A divorce went against everything I'd ever believed in. I valued my marriage vows and worked at being a friend, a lover, a helper, and companion to my husband. While I gave my whole self to him, he betrayed me and refused to nurture and commit to a vow that he made before God.

Sometimes the anger and hurt overwhelm me.

Because of love for her children and herself, Tessa knew she had to do something. She couldn't continue to live in a pit of despair and poverty. Frantically, she cried out to God for direction. She had to provide for her children and find a purpose for her life.

In the past, Tessa had entertained the idea of teaching school on the elementary level, but the opportunity never arose. After her divorce, she was free to pursue teaching if she wanted to. The only catch was, she would have to go to college. Tessa was in her early thirties with a family to raise. The impossibilities loomed heavy over her, but with humility and great determination Tessa and her children moved in with her father and she enrolled in college. "Having a loving and supportive family who helped with the kids and allowed us to stay in their home was a major factor in my recovery process," Tessa told me.

"Going back to school built up my self-confidence," she continued. My old dream of being the perfect wife, mother, and homemaker died. It was actually dead long before I was able to let it go. To move forward in a healthy way, I had to develop a new dream."

Tessa knew she had made mistakes in her past. Now she wanted to do more than just *not* make the same mistakes again. Tessa didn't want to make *any* mistakes at all. She resolved to herself, "I'm going to find out how to do things 'right' this time." Thus, Tessa began a journey to find out how to have a successful, normal life. "If," she told me, "I could just find out what normal was."

At this point, she had given up on the pursuit of having a healthy romantic relationship. She had been betrayed, and she never wanted to feel that kind of pain again. She was her own woman now and would determine her own path. Tessa's resolve to be a loving mother never changed, but her dream switched from being a quaint homemaker to being a successful teacher. Her grades were high, and she worked diligently and passionately. Tessa's confidence soared: "I just knew I was going to be a wonderful teacher. After all, I was attending one of the best elementary-education schools in the state, and I had a deep love for children. Who wouldn't want to hire me?"

As Tessa envisioned her future as a teacher, she pictured in her mind a traditional classroom, just like in the movies—decorated in bright primary colors, with neat children who said, "Gooood mooornnning, Ms. Tesssaaa!" All smart kids, with caring and involved parents, eager and willing to learn, like little sponges soaking up all the knowledge she would give them.

After graduation, though, Tessa could not find a job. She searched and scoured, but nothing opened up. Finally, out of desperation, she interviewed at an inner-city school located in a crime-ridden, drug-infested part of town and was hired to teach the first grade. "It was the only job offered to me, so I had to take it," she told me.

When Tessa began teaching, once again her dream of what her life "should be" was shattered. "Most of these kids came to school with *no* supplies. Their parents are in dire poverty. They didn't want to learn. I had to spend hours teaching them to behave, before I could teach them anything else. Many of my students are abused or neglected. Three of my students' parents are in jail. A significant percent are crack babies, which causes super-hyperactivity. One of them brought a gun to school—in the first grade! Another one had ringworm and had patches the size of cup lids all over his body."

Each day, after work, Tessa cried. She bought news-papers and continued diligently to look for a new job. But it was as though a steel door had been slammed shut. There were just no jobs to be had. In desperation Tessa prayed, "God, I can't do this! I went to school for noth-ing. If I can't do this, then I can't do anything!"

Tessa felt like a failure. She had failed first at mar-riage and now as a teacher, and she didn't want to go back into that classroom. Tessa was so miserable, she says, "I was driving those around me crazy. Facing each new day became harder and harder until one day I came to the end of my rope, again."

That day, after many prayers, a light switched on in her head. God showed her that she was trying to fit her students into her expectations of what "normal" was supposed to be. Tessa determined not to give up on her job just yet, or on her students, but to press on. "After a while," she told me, "I began to change. Now I know it wasn't the children who needed to change; it was me." She started seeing her students as individuals, who had individual problems. "I was the only person some of these kids had who offered them any positive emotional support."

Tessa implemented a system in which at the beginning of each day each of her students had to greet her by either shaking her hand, slapping her a high five, or giving her a hug. In the beginning, most of the kids were emotionally guarded because too many people in their lives had let them down, and most didn't want anything to do with touching her. However, through Tessa's continual praise and the unconditional acceptance she offered, they slowly began to open up. Now, almost every one of them gives her, not high fives, but hugs. "Some don't want to let me go," Tessa told me. "It may be the only hug they get all day. But they had to learn to trust me."

Tessa has seen such a change in her students and herself that she now knows that God took her idealistic dream of teaching and turned it into a very realistic *calling* to reach these children in need. As the principal of the school says, "I know that God sent Tessa to our school." Tessa responds to the principal's compliment by saying "Yes, God put me in this school, but it was as much for me as for them." Wow, what a turnaround!

The wisdom Tessa gained can be applied to all our lives. Listen to her own words:

I still have my bad days. But at the end of each day I have peace knowing I'm where God wants me. Instead of crying like I used to, I laugh a lot.

What I've learned, and what I'm filtering down to my students, is that life is about taking risks. We don't always know the outcome, but regardless of our past or present situation, we must have the self-confidence to step out.

My classroom is not what I envisioned in college and there's always a shortage of funding, but my life is more rewarding than it has ever been. In my classroom, as in my personal life, I kept waiting for everything to be perfect. Finally, I realized I had to take a leap of faith, which meant trusting people and God again.

I know there are no guarantees, but I also know if I am a whole person, secure in God and myself, then I will always make it. That gives me great hope for the future—a realistic hope. I know, from experience, that God can take our broken dreams and unfulfilled expectations and use them if we let Him. Then our lives will be complete.

Most of us desperately want life to fit into our ideas of how things *should* be. We consider a bump in the road to be a negative thing. But sometimes there are surprising riches in the detours we are forced to take to get around that bump.

One of my favorite ways of looking at this comes

from Joyce Meyer's book *Managing Your Emotions*. She wrote, "When we are disappointed . . . we have to make the decision to adopt and adjust, to take a new approach, to keep going despite our feelings. That's when we must remember that we have the greater One residing within us, so that no matter what happens to us, we can let God turn our disappointment into a reappointment!"[42]

I love this concept of letting God reappoint us when life hands us disappointments. It's something I've used throughout my own experiences.

My friend Tessa had many disappointments, but in her pain, she let God reappoint her to a much greater task than she could have ever imagined. She told herself, "I'll dream a new dream as my old life fades into a memory."

Today, Tessa is engaged to be married to a wonderfully supportive and encouraging man. In that relationship also, Tessa has had to learn to let go of her past and trust again. Though it is difficult, with God's help she's doing it.

Disappointments are inevitable in life—even in a "normal" life. This fact of life, however, doesn't have to be a negative. Sometimes closed doors, failure, and disappointment can become the greatest avenues for blessings. I firmly believe that when God closes a door, He opens a window or another door better suited for us.

The quote at the beginning of this chapter from Billy Joel, the famous pop singer, is quite astounding to me. When I first read it, it caught me somewhat off guard because I've always held a particular image in my mind of pop singers. Billy Joel's story shattered my preconceived image of him. His story is another choice example of turning disappointment into reappointment.

Growing up, Billy Joel had eleven years of classical piano training, and his big dream was to write and perform symphonies like Beethoven. He pursued his dream with a passion but kept making blunders and foul-ups. Finally, he realized that he would never be another Beethoven. Yet his foul-ups are what helped him find his own unique style of music. In a commencement speech at Fairfield University in Fairfield, Connecticut, he said:

> *I have learned that my strengths are a result of my weaknesses, my success is due to my failures, and my style is directly related to my limitations.*
>
> *I have discovered that after all those years of musical instruction, after all that practice to be perfect, after all that hard work trying to compose the right notes, I am gifted with the knack of hitting exactly the wrong notes at precisely the right time.*
>
> *This is the secret of originality. Think about it . . . Only you can commit a colossal blunder in your own exquisite style. This is what makes you unique. But when you are faced with solving the problem, this is what makes you inventive.*[43]

Tessa reappointed her disappointments. So did Billy Joel. Both are now living lives beyond their own limited expectations. The next time you find yourself in a disappointing situation, don't give in to depression and fear. Instead, give in to God and let Him reappoint you.

7.

All I Need
Is a Miracle

O My soul, don't be discouraged. Don't be upset.
Expect God to act! . . . He is my help! He is my
God!

—PSALM 42:11, LIVING BIBLE

A ll I need is a miracle . . ." Although those are the
words of a popular rock 'n' roll song, to some of us
they have become our heart's cry. "If God would just do
this one thing for me, then my life would be fine. If I
could only have a miracle, then I would believe." Are you
sure? Would you?

Miracles. The mere mention of the word invokes all
sorts of images. To some, miracles are those rare occurrences in time when God supernaturally overrules the
fixed laws of the universe. Some feel that everything in
life is a miracle, from the mighty oak tree that grows out

of a tiny seed to the birth of a child. And to others, well, miracles just don't happen. To give credence to them would be letting emotionalism overrule what our rational minds believe to be true.

I'm acutely aware that when the subject of miracles is brought up, one frequently thinks of those people who live in La La Land. You know, those who are out of touch with reality—people who walk around as if they were floating on clouds or something. You know what I mean. Just the other day on the national news I saw a show about those attending what were called "miracle cults."

As a believer in God, a follower of Christ, and an advocate for the power of prayer, I get frustrated when intelligent levelheaded believers in God's power get lumped together with those who are obviously unbalanced. Believing in miracles can be a sensible and rational thing.

I've also seen deeply faithful, balanced people die, not having received their much wanted and much needed miracle. My friend Ben is a good example. Around the time my writing and speaking career began to take off and a lot of good things were happening in my life, Ben found out he had terminal cancer. Ben and I were almost the same age. He had a beautiful wife and two lovely daughters, ages four and six. Ben and I attended the same men's Bible study group. Each week, with a smile on his face, he told the group how he was asking God for his recovery. In addition to prayer, Ben religiously followed his doctor's orders. Our group prayed daily for Ben's recovery; but instead of getting better, each week Ben got weaker and weaker. As his pain intensified, so did our prayers. But not once did we see Ben complain or murmur.

It was during Ben's bout with cancer that I had my first major book signing. Over three hundred people came out to wish me well. Ben and his family were right there in line offering their support. As Ben approached my table, he was smiling from ear to ear, genuinely happy for my success. If there ever was a godly man, it was Ben. I signed his book and commented on his lovely family. We squeezed each other's hands tightly, and unspoken warmth flowed through us. He looked at me in a way that seemed to pierce my heart. I could see his discomfort and weariness. It was as if Ben were saying good-bye to me, but without the words. I never saw Ben again. He died a short time later. After his death, I asked God, "Why didn't Ben get a miracle?" You've done so much in my life, God. Yet Ben, who really needed a miracle, who had three people dependent on him, died. Why, God?"

The plain truth is this: Miracles don't always happen. But sometimes they do. And according to the quotation from Scripture at the beginning of this chapter, we are supposed to "expect God to act!" I feel it would be a disservice to God, if I did not include the miracle aspect of God's power in my writings.

For years, I have been intrigued with the phenomenon of the *miracle,* which the new Random House unabridged dictionary defines as "an effect or extraordinary event in the physical world that bypasses all human or natural powers and is ascribed to a supernatural cause" or "such an effect or event manifesting or considered as a work of God—a wonder or marvel." I studied miracles in seminary and in the years that followed, doing extensive research and even interviewing people who had experienced authentic miracles. I came across enough incredible miraculous stories that my faith was forever altered. The supernatural occurrences I've both seen in others and personally experienced give me the encouragement to know that even when I don't receive a notable miracle in a trying situation, I know God is still in control and has a reason for what I am experiencing.

A major step in transcending our storms and anchoring our soul is, first, believing that God exists and, second, that He is personally involved in our lives. It is a mystery to me how God can be personally involved with billions of people all at the same time. Logically, it seems impossible. On the other hand, the commonsense evidence in the world pointing to a *personal* God is so overwhelming that by today's litigation standards, if God were on trial for His existence, He would be found guilty beyond any reasonable doubt.

Former agnostic Pamela Ewen has been an attorney and a partner for over twenty years in the international law firm Baker & Botts, with offices in New York, Washington, D.C., and London. Inspired by previous scholars such as Simon Greenleaf and by her own personal search for faith, Ewen started researching the evidence for a rational basis for the existence of a *personal* God. As a result she wrote the book *Faith on Trial* (Broadman & Holman). In it, Pamela held the evidence to the same standards as any other testimony within a U.S. court of law. She assumes the burden of proof in the case. As a result of Pamela's findings, she is no longer an agnostic. Instead, she is a committed believer.

Take all the evidence for God in creation and history. Add to it the millions of genuine accounts of miracles that are out there, some of which I'm about to share with you, and it clearly indicates that God is real and that He is, in fact, personally involved in our lives.

I do not claim to be a scholar or to have all the answers regarding this subject. I get baffled at God's ways just as much as the next guy. Remember, I have a deaf son. However, in my research, I've uncovered what seems to be a pattern regarding supernatural events. The pattern works something like this:

1. Most of the time (though not always), miracles happen after a person believes, *not* before. God desires us to walk in faith. If we are seeking a miracle merely to convince us of His existence, it rarely happens. God has left enough evidence around for us to come to a conclusion to begin to trust Him.

2. Most of the miracles I've seen have come in two ways: either by God's sovereign intervention or through a prompting, from Him. In the first instance, the miracle just happened. The recipient wasn't seeking it. In the second instance, a person "heard" a prompting from God in his heart and, by faith, followed that prompting, and God performed a miracle. Now, a person must make sure he's hearing from God and not merely his emotions. God would

rarely lead someone to do something that goes against His nature or our God-given common sense. For example, you may believe God is going to heal your body from a particular illness. That doesn't mean you are to throw away your medication or stop taking the doctor's advice. There are cases, few though, when the medication and treatment were actually making people sick, and they felt led by God to get off it and became better. But for the most part, we should use our common sense.

3. God gives us miracles in two ways: The majority of the time, He gives us supernatural strength and peace to dig through our mountains, developing depth of character as we dig. Sometimes, people who don't receive obvious miracles but continue to be faithful throughout their trials, even in death, become tools to reach other hurting people. Having peace amid the storm and removing the sting of death are still the greatest miracles of all. Yet, sometimes God does overrule the natural laws and supernaturally removes the mountain.

True faith says, "Whatever route God takes me, I will triumph." My goal in this chapter is not to try to convert you or lead you in a particular way, but simply to share some incredible miraculous stories with you that I believe will strengthen you as you face life's challenges. My hope is that these miracles will cause you to seek God, not miracles.

To the skeptics, I insist that the stories I'm about to share with you are not exaggerations. As a realist and a critical thinker, I have gone to great lengths not to exaggerate. The people spoken of in this chapter, like Ken Gaub, for example, with whom I personally spoke, had no motivation to make up tall tales. Many are quiet people just like you and I, but their lives have been significantly changed by miracles. In my personal study of miracles, I wanted to find the truth, not just stories that would support what I already believed.

So why is it so important to read the stories of other peoples' miracles? Faith and strength come through the testimony of others' experiences. In my personal life, I can't tell you how many times when I needed faith to make it through tough situations I've drawn upon what I've seen God do in other people and in my own life. During times in my life, usually when God seems silent and I'm experiencing difficulty, I'll pray a prayer similar to this condensed one: "God, I know you are real because I can see all the evidence around me. I know you are real because of the undeniable miracles I've seen you perform for others and myself. I know what happened could not have been mere coincidence. God, I don't understand what I'm going through, but I know you are real. And if you are real, that means you have a reason for your silence and what I'm going through. Father, I choose to trust you." During my prayer, in my mind I will go over in detail the incredible events I've seen at the hand of God. I also lean heavily on the promises of God revealed in Scripture, such as: *"Though I am surrounded by troubles, you will bring me safely through them"* (Psalm 138:7) or *"Do not fear, for I am with you; do not anxiously look about you, for I am your God. I will strengthen you, surely I will help you"* (Isaiah 41:10). Drawing upon God's miracles can be a source of empowerment during your dark times.

Miracles of Provision

The Guitar

While studying journalism at the University of Mississippi, I experienced an extraordinary event that I could not dismiss as a mere coincidence.

One night, during the Christmas break, I began my regular prayer routine. As I prayed, something happened in my inner mind. It's hard to explain, but a voice, a still small voice, permeated my inner mind saying "Give your guitar away." At this time, I was interested in playing the guitar and singing. So understand, this was *not* something I wanted to hear or do. I didn't have much money, and giving away a five hundred-dollar guitar would mean I would be without one for the foreseeable future.

I went to bed trying to dismiss this thought, but the more I wished it away, the stronger it became. I dozed off. When I picked up my guitar the next morning, boom, the thought came back. For days, every time I picked up my guitar, that thought nagged me. It just wouldn't leave me alone. Finally I said, "Okay, God, you win. I'll give my guitar away. So who do I give it to?" No sooner did I ask than a name popped into my head: John Edwards. I was puzzled because I didn't know John that well. Nor did I know if he had any interest in guitars. He attended a campus Bible study class that I also attended and never gave me any indication that he was interested in music.

When classes resumed after the semester break, I looked John up. When we met I said, "John, you may think I'm crazy, but God wants me to give you this guitar. If you don't play, keep it anyway." I was expecting John to look at me as if I had lost my mind, but to my surprise, tears filled his eyes. Then, right there, on the spot, he pulled out of his book bag a personal journal and told me that over the holidays, while in prayer, God had spoken to his inner being as well and told him to write down the following words. As long as I live, I will never forget those words. I can quote them, because I've reflected on them hundreds, maybe thousands, of times through the years . . .

> *There is a guitar, which I, the Lord, God, am going to give you. Though you do not know how to play, I will teach you to play and sing praises to me.*

John believed that if the inner voice that compelled him to write those words were God's, then somehow, God would give him a guitar. Then, without any knowledge of what God had told John, I sought him out and gave him my guitar that I didn't even want to give away.

You have got to believe me when I say I had *no* idea that John was even remotely interested in playing the guitar. In fact, he had never played a lick, until I gave him my guitar!

Both John and I were amazed. Neither of us understood why God had done what He did, but we absolutely knew He was real and personally involved in our lives.

A Girl's Watch

Dr. Paul Yonggi Cho is founder and pastor of a church in Seoul, Korea. When Dr. Cho began to build his church, he was living in dire poverty in a one-room hovel with a dirt floor. The sum of his belongings consisted of a few bits of well-used clothing, a desk and a chair, some eating utensils, study books, and a bicycle. It was also during this time that Dr. Cho became engaged to his future wife. In a moment of excitement, he pledged to buy his fiancée a new watch to commemorate their engagement. He told her he would have it for her the next time they saw each other, which would be the following Monday.

But when Dr. Cho began to calculate his net assets, he realized he had spoken in haste. In Korea, if a person makes a pledge, he is expected to fulfill it or be disgraced. Even though it was just a watch, seemingly a small thing, Dr. Cho was in a real predicament. "How could I expect her to marry me," he wondered, "after I did not keep my promise?"

For several days, Dr. Cho prayed to God to provide

him with a watch for his future wife. He remembers specifically praying, "Father, you are the great provider. You provided for Abraham. Won't you be my provider?" Dr. Cho said a peace came to his heart, and though he didn't know how, he knew that God had the answer. He made a decision to trust God and tell no one of his need. Eventually, Sunday night rolled around and still no watch. This was during the Korean War, and Seoul had a midnight curfew. No one could leave his home after twelve o'clock until morning. Dr. Cho began to worry, and desperately he began to pray. As he did, says Dr. Cho, "a peace again came to my heart. I knew that God had the answer and had made provision. I was going to trust Him, yet my mind was paying attention to the clock on the wall. Within a few minutes, the curfew would be in effect..." Just before midnight, someone knocked on his door. It was an American soldier. The soldier said, "Pastor Cho, I have a real problem. . . . You see, I have a niece back home in America. Next week is her birthday. Well, on Friday, I bought her a wristwatch. It is a really nice one and I got it for a good price at the PX. My problem is this: Tonight, I was wrapping it up and God's spirit began to speak to me. He said I'm to give the watch to you ... but I know you are a man and have no need for a girl's watch. What can I do?"

After Dr. Cho explained his situation, the soldier got so excited that he began to dance around yelling, "God really used me! God really used me!" Dr. Cho thanked God for making provision in a way that he could never have imagined.[44]

A Heavenly Message

Linda Smith's young son, Alex,* was accidentally shot and killed while he was visiting a friend's house. Several boys were playing, and one of them found a loaded gun and started passing it around. When the gun was handed, barrel first, to Alex, it discharged, sending a bullet into his chest and killing him almost instantly.

For Linda, losing her son was devastating. Yet, a pre-death vision Alex had had two months prior to his death had given her hope that Alex's death had a purpose. Linda says, "His death has taught many people about life."

Two months before his death, Alex came to the breakfast table looking tired, as if he had not slept all night. When Linda asked what was wrong, he said that he'd had a very vivid dream. A tall woman dressed in white "like a glowing princess" had come to him and told him that time was running short. All the doors around him in this dream closed, and the only place left to go was down a long hallway.

"And that was it," Alex said. "It was weird."

Throughout the following weeks he had recurrences of this same dream and began drawing pictures of objects that appeared to him during the dream. One object was a tall, very peculiarly shaped monument. Another was a tree with branches in a certain formation. Alex did not know what the drawings meant, but he continued to produce them and ask his parents for their

*Names have been changed.

opinion. Linda wrote about them in her journal and even collected some of the drawings.

Two days before he was shot, Alex and Linda went for a walk. He took Linda's hand and said in the most serious tone: "If I die, don't cry about it. I know I'm going to be happy there because they showed me. It's beautiful."

Linda was shocked. She asked Alex pointedly if he was thinking of committing suicide, which he denied. "I just don't think I'm going to be here much longer," he responded.

Two days later, Alex was shot. When he was buried, Linda and her husband noticed two things at the grave site that they had seen on his drawing pads: the tall, peculiarly shaped monument from a neighboring grave and the tree with a particular branch pattern.[45]

This story points out that though we may not understand why certain things happen, they still have a purpose. Our natural minds see losing a child as a tragedy, and to those left behind the pain is real. Yet, as this story confirms, God knows things that we don't.

A Miraculous Healing

Herb Mjorud's story is a remarkable account of a documented healing of terminal cancer. Herb, a pastor, was diagnosed with incurable lymphoma in 1980. The cancer had metastasized, and malignant cells were moving all through his body. The principal tumor was planting seeds of itself.

Not giving up, Herb Mjorud began to fill his mind with Scripture about God's healing power. He prayed fervently for a complete recovery, but nothing changed for the better. The cancer continued to progress. After several months, it became clear that the chemotherapy with which he was being treated was not reducing the growth of the tumor. Herb Mjorud was a dying man.

During this time, God spoke to Herb and said, "Spend three days in prayer and praise and on the third day, I will do something." Herb had little doubt that he had heard from God, but the chemotherapy had destroyed his voice and he was so weak he couldn't even speak, let alone praise God. If you have ever been around people in the final stages of cancer, you know that they are reduced to almost a mere skin-covered skeleton. They can't hold down food or water and usually are in great pain. They are so weak that the slightest activity, even speaking, is too much. Herb was in this stage. Death was not months, but only days, away.

But for three days, hour after hour, he listened to his favorite worship tape, mouthing the voice of the singers as his own. Then, on the third day, once again he heard the voice of God—this time, even stronger: "Do what I did to the fig tree. Read Mark, chapter 11." In that chapter, Jesus had cursed a fruitless fig tree, and the tree withered and died. Herb felt the message was that the tumor was going to wither and die as the fig tree had. In a whisper, he thanked God for cursing the tumor down to its roots. Instantly, at that very moment, Herb's voice returned to full strength. And so did his appetite. For days, he ate heartily and was able to hold down the food. When his oncologist examined him and tested his blood, the doctor had no alternative but to say that there was no cancer, that without a doubt Herb had received a miracle. Herb Mjorud has been free of cancer for over fourteen years.[46]

God Knows Right Where You Are

When I first heard this astounding account, I must admit, I too was somewhat skeptical. Initially, I hesitated to include it in the book. But as I researched it, I realized that if this story were indeed true, then its implications were far-reaching. The more I researched, the more validity the story had. First, I tracked down Ken Gaub, whom the story is about. I found him to be a real person, with an actual address and phone number. This miraculous event absolutely changed his life and lifestyle. He has smuggled Bibles into communist countries. He has been shot at, put in jail, and lives out of a suitcase so he can share his story around the world. He's not a wealthy man. In fact, he could have made much more money doing something else. With each mission trip he takes, he depends on God for physical strength and for finances. When I talked with him, Ken was praying for God to provide him with a van. Does that sound like a wealthy man? This man had absolutely no motive to make up a story like this. It's the miracle he experienced and his relationship with God that keep him doing what he does. One doesn't live a life like Ken Gaub lives on the basis of a lie.

Another thing that convinced me to include this story was the fact that many credible people endorse Ken, some that I know personally. Also, his wife and family are involved with his ministry. They know firsthand of the account. In addition, the story has been on the television series *Unsolved Mysteries* and *It's a Miracle*. As you read it, let this awesome account reach down into the depths of your soul and give you hope.

Again, I can't say why God reveals Himself to some in this fashion and to others He seems silent. However, if anyone can read this true story and still doubt that God is a personal God, then they doubt by shear stubbornness.

It had always been Ken Gaub's goal to help those who were hurting. "Some people just need a little boost, and I wanted to influence their lives in a positive way," he says. He became a traveling missionary and, with his family, conducted services not only throughout America but also in many foreign countries.

But sometimes even preachers get drained and discouraged, and they wonder if they should consider another line of work. That was how Ken felt one day in the 1970s as he, his wife, Barbara, and their children drove their two ministry buses down I-75 just south of Dayton, Ohio. "God, am I doing any good, traveling around like this, telling people about You?" Ken wondered silently. "Is this what you want me to do?"

"Hey, Dad, let's get some pizza!" one of Ken's sons suggested. Still lost in thought, Ken turned off at the next exit, Route 741, where one sign after another advertised a wide variety of fast food. "A sign," Ken mused. "That's what I need from You, God, a sign."

Ken's son and daughter-in-law had already maneuvered the second bus into a pizza parlor's parking lot, and they stood waiting as Ken pulled up. The rest of the family bounced down the steps. Ken sat staring into space.

"Coming?" Barbara asked.

"I'm not really hungry," Ken told her. "I'll stay out here and stretch my legs."

Barbara followed the others into the restaurant, and Ken stepped outside, closed the bus doors, and looked around. Noticing a Dairy Queen, he strolled over, bought a soft drink, and ambled back, still pondering. He was exhausted. But were his doldrums a sign of permanent burnout?

A persistent ringing broke Ken's concentration. The jangle was coming from a pay telephone in a booth at the service station right next to the Dairy Queen. As Ken approached the booth, he looked to see if anyone in the station was coming to answer it. But the attendant continued his work, seemingly oblivious to the noise. "Why doesn't someone answer it?" Ken wondered, growing irritated. "What if it's an emergency?"

The insistent ringing went on. Ten rings. Fifteen . . . Curiosity overcame Ken's lethargy. Walking to the booth, he lifted the receiver. "Hello?"

"Long-distance call for Ken Gaub," came the voice of the operator.

Ken was stunned. "You're crazy!" he said. Then, realizing his rudeness, he tried to explain. "This can't be! I was just walking down the road here, and the phone was ringing . . ."

The operator ignored his ramblings. "Is Ken Gaub there?" she asked. "I have a long-distance phone call for him."

Was this a joke? Automatically, Ken smoothed his hair for the *Candid Camera* crew that must surely appear.

But no one came. His family was eating pizza in a randomly selected restaurant just a few yards from where he stood. And no one else knew he was here.

"I have a long-distance call for Ken Gaub, sir," the operator said again, obviously reaching the limits of her patience. "Is he there or isn't he?"

"Operator, I'm Ken Gaub," Ken said, still unable to make sense of it.

"Are you sure?" the operator asked, but just then, Ken heard another woman's voice on the telephone.

"Yes, that's him, Operator!" she said. "Mr. Gaub, I'm Millie from Harrisburg, Pennsylvania. You don't know me, but I'm desperate. Please help me."

"What can I do for you?" Ken asked. The operator hung up.

Millie began to weep, and Ken waited patiently for her to regain control. Finally she explained. "I was about to kill myself, and I started to write a suicide note. Then I began to pray and tell God I really didn't want to do this . . ." Through her desolation, Millie remembered seeing Ken on television. If she could just talk to that nice, kindly minister, the one with the understanding attitude . . . "I knew it was impossible because I didn't know how to reach you," Millie went on, calmer now. "So I started to finish the note. And then some numbers came into my mind, and I wrote them down." She began to weep again. Silently Ken prayed for the wisdom to help her.

"I looked at those numbers," Millie continued tearfully, "and I thought—wouldn't it be wonderful if I had a miracle from God, and He has given me Ken's phone number?" I can't believe I'm talking to you. Are you in your office in California?"

"I don't have an office in California," Ken explained. "It's in Yakima, Washington."

"Then where are you?" Millie asked puzzled.

Ken was even more bewildered. "Millie, don't you know? You made the call."

"But I don't know what area this is." Millie had dialed the long distance operator, making it a person-to-person call, and given the numbers to her. And somehow she had found Ken in a parking lot in Dayton, Ohio.

Ken gently counseled the woman. Soon she met the One who would lead her out of her situation into a new life. Then he hung up the phone, still dazed. Would his family believe this incredible story? Perhaps he shouldn't tell anyone about it.

But he had prayed for an answer, and he had received just what he needed—a renewed sense of purpose, a glimpse of the value of his work, an electrifying awareness of God's concern for each of His children—all in an encounter that could only have been arranged by His heavenly Father.[47]

My Incredible Story
You must read this one!

As I write the following account, please know that a deep sense of humility fills my heart. My story is rare and certainly miraculous, but I cannot take any credit for its unfolding. I simply followed what I felt was God's obvious lead. I've shared this same story with audiences everywhere, and each time I do, many people are left in tears. My prayer is that it will also affect you—that it will point you to a God that is, no doubt, personally involved in our lives, even when circumstances leave us feeling otherwise. The story is a bit lengthy, but please hear it out; I believe you will be glad you did.

The book you are reading right now is a miracle. I don't write that casually, either. This is not one of those sweet you-can-be-whatever-you-want-to-be motivational stories. No, by the same definition as the others, this really is an authentic miracle, or series of miracles. My whole career as a writer is a miracle. My life is a miracle.

Let me explain. In 1977, I was a fairly typical seventeen-year-old boy. My life was wrapped up in football, cars, and girls. I was an all-state football player. I drove a Grand Torino Sport, just like the one Starsky and Hutch had in the old TV series. My grades were slightly below average, mainly because I rarely studied. I loathed reading. I loathed school. Sitting in class was torture. I now know that I am severely affected by attention deficit disorder, but back then we didn't know what ADD was. The only thing that kept me interested in school was sports and friends.

Soon, though, my life took a dramatic turn. Through a highly respected friend and a certain chain of events, I made a serious commitment to follow God and Christ. The changes in my personality as a result of my resolve were immediate and lasting. It was obvious to me, and to others, that Max Davis was a new person. Yes, I was still a teenager who played football, drove a cool car, and liked girls. But now I had a connection with God that I hadn't had before. He was real to me.

Then one night, while I was driving down the road, it happened. I was simply driving along, when a thought just leaped into my mind. The thought was: "You are going to be an author of books." Get this—that thought had to have come from God, because it surely didn't come from me. The last things on my mind were books and reading. Heck, I wasn't even sure if my grade-point average was good enough for me to get into college. Now something or someone was telling me that I was going to be an author! That would definitely take a miracle.

After that, the seed to be a writer was placed in my soul. Just as the thought of giving away my guitar nagged me, so this thought of being a writer nagged at me as well. It's hard to explain. Though I had no idea how it was going to happen, I did know, deep down in my soul, that I was going to be an author one day.

Now, in my undeveloped, seventeen-year-old mind, I figured it was going to happen right then. So I did what I thought I was supposed to do: I started writing. My girlfriend, who was an art student, helped me design a book cover for my best-seller. All this while I was barely passing English! My writing was horrible, but I was convinced that God had spoken to me.

At the time, I lived in the country, close to a winding river, and I would go for long walks along its sandy banks, talk to God, and read the Scriptures for hours on end. Many times, during those walks, I saw myself speaking to large groups via television and radio. I would practice speaking to imaginary audiences, giving interviews about my imaginary books. Understand, all this was happening when I was seventeen years old! It wasn't an ego trip because I didn't have the knowledge then about television and radio and book promotion. All this was coming out of my heart. God was planting seeds. But most important, Christ was becoming my best friend and my source of strength.

My senior year passed and I continued to write, holding on to my God-given dream. When I graduated, I was blessed with an offer to play football at the University of Mississippi on a full scholarship. My GPA was a 2.0, and I was accepted on academic probation. This meant I had to maintain a 2.5 GPA to keep my scholarship. Because of my call to write and speak, I figured the best thing to do would be to major in journalism, which I thought would help develop my writing and speaking skills.

All through my undergraduate years, whenever I went to a mall, I would head for the bookstore and browse, dreaming of the day when my book would be on the shelves. Every time I saw an author speaking, I imagined myself doing the same thing. The seed God planted in me was beginning to grow. It was also during this time I got married. I was so serious about my writing that my first apartment had to have a room for my desk and typewriter. As time passed, little by little, my writing began to improve. Also, I was starting to believe in my intelligence. By my senior year I made the dean's list!

After graduation, I could not find a job in journalism and wound up back home, working for my dad as an air conditioner repairman. Yet, I still had a room where I continued to write. For two years, I struggled with this deep call to be a writer and speaker, but saw no possible way it could come to pass. I was so frustrated. I went for many long walks at night, crying out to God. I told Him something to this effect: "God, I know that You called me to be an author. I can't explain it. I just know it. I've been writing now for over six years and nothing is happening. I don't know what to do. Please tell me." Over the next few weeks, it became evident that I was supposed to go back to school and work on a master's degree in theology and counseling. My plan was to combine my journalism skills with my theology and counseling. I had a wife and a baby, but we made the move out of state, to Tulsa, Oklahoma, so I could attend seminary.

While attending seminary, I worked the early-morning shift at United Parcel Service and went to classes in the afternoons. My friends knew my desire to be a writer. One friend even gave me a book for Christmas and inside wrote, "Your writing will one day surpass [a certain famous author] because you heart does." Just as I kept my writings from my high school years, I also kept this book. Soon professors were confirming my gift. One of the most difficult professors wrote on the back of a thesis: "Max, your writing is alive." Imagine the boost those few words gave me! My skills were growing, and so was my knowledge.

But soon I graduated, and still nothing happened. I wound up as a truck driver for UPS in Tulsa. I had now spent ten years pursuing this calling with nothing to show for it, except a career as a truck driver. The money was good and I was getting settled into the family routine. I had no idea how my call to write and speak was going to come to pass. Still, I continued to work at it. I was compelled to write. God wouldn't let me stop. As I drove my truck, I carried a notebook by my side. On my route there were a couple of bookstores. They were my favorite stops. I always took more time on those. This went on for three more years. Then, my second child, James, was born. Thirteen months later, we found out about his deafness.

Enter Miracle Series #1

One night I had a vivid dream. I was pastoring a small church. It was so real, as if I were watching a movie. A banner across the top of the church read LAWRENCE, KANSAS. When I woke up, I thought it was weird. Lawrence, Kansas, had no relevance to me. It could as well have been Bend, Oregon, or Albuquerque, New Mexico. What did it mean? Being the type of guy that I am, I brushed it off as simply a weird dream. "Maybe I ate too much pizza," I thought, jokingly.

The following Saturday, I took James and my daughter Kristen to the city park. Tulsa is a city of about 500,000, and there were hundreds of people there. As I was pushing James on a swing and talking to him in sign language, a woman, whom I'd never seen before, walked up to me and said, "I see your son is deaf." After a few minutes of conversation, she said straightforwardly, "You need to get that boy to Lawrence, Kansas. They have a great program for the deaf there." As you can imagine, my jaw almost hit the ground. Could my dream and this incident with a total stranger be mere coincidence?

When I got back home, I called my pastor and asked if we could meet. I told him of the two strange occurrences. Then I asked him if he thought God was telling me to move to Lawrence. It could be God, he told me, but only time would tell. Well, time did tell, in a matter of days!

Two or three days after the meeting with my pastor, he received a letter in the mail from a small, brand-new church in—you guessed it—Lawrence, Kansas. The letter requested a charter for the church to join our denomination and also asked my pastor if he knew of anyone who might be interested in coming there to lead the church. My pastor immediately forwarded the information to me. After hearing my story, the denomination headquarters agreed to pay me a nice salary to go to Lawrence and help get this church up and running. Within a few short weeks, my family was living in Lawrence and I was pastoring the church, a church strangely similar to the one in my dream. And James was enrolled in a top-notch program for the deaf. A mere coincidence? You tell me.

So here I was, pastoring this church, and the call to it was so convincing that I just knew I would have great success. Yet, the urge to write just kept nagging at me. In my mind, I had everything all figured out. I could do both, be a pastor and an author. I began to write more diligently than ever. My congregation became guinea pigs for my chapters. Each time I wrote something, I would give it to several of my members and ask their opinions. The first year or so everything was great. The church was growing. We grew through three buildings.

I purchased a beautiful house. Life couldn't have been better, but storm clouds loomed on the horizon.

Soon my life changed, yet again, in a way I'd never dreamed possible. And I learned that God's ways are not always our ways and that He is working in our lives even when we feel as though He is not.

For several months, I could sense things around the house were not right. I couldn't put my finger on what was wrong, though. There was a tension in the air. When I thought about it, I would quickly dismiss the thought and say things to myself like "Everything's okay. It must be because you're doing God's work." But things were not okay, and soon I found myself in the midst of a painful divorce. I felt completely blindsided. I had seen so much success in my life. Nearly everything I had set out to accomplish I had done. My future was heading in the right direction. I had life all figured out. My plans were laid. Yet, I was so wrapped up in realizing my own vision and in counseling other people that I had unknowingly put my family in second place.

In a matter of months, my great life came tumbling down. I lost everything: the new house, my job as a pastor (I resigned so I could focus on my family), and most important, I was separated from my children. Then, to top things off, I had trouble finding an adequate job, and my expenses from the divorce and child support were taking what money I had each month. For months, I was homeless, unable to afford an apartment of my own. Several nights, I slept on the side of the road in my car. Once I was awakened in the morning by the sound of a policeman banging on the car window. I wound up living with friends for a long time.

After a while, my ex-wife moved back to Louisiana, and I followed to be close to my kids. Crushed, humiliated, poor, and broken, I moved home with my parents without a clue of what to do with my life. I was totally confused.

I was an achiever. How could I have ended up as a total failure? All my personal dreams had died. The idea of being a writer was long gone. My central concern became that of seeing my children and supporting myself.

The more I searched for a good job, however, the worse things got. I tried getting back my UPS job, but even with my experience, they were not hiring permanent drivers. So, I sold vacuum cleaners. I sold cars. I sold insurance. I painted houses. I collected scrap metal from junk air-conditioning units and sold it. None of these are bad jobs; it's just that I wasn't making any money and I was getting further into debt. I was borrowing money from my dad to put gas in my twelve-year-old car!

Eventually, I hit bottom. I mean, rock bottom—totally broken—and I'm here to say, it was the best thing that ever happened to me. How can I say that? Well it's true, because God is faithful, not me. Life was *not* good. But God *is* good.

When I hit bottom, I remember making a conscious choice to stop trying to control and blame my ex-wife for my problems and turn control over to God. In tears, I told God that no matter what happened in my future, I was going to serve Him and trust Him and that I just wanted to be a good father. When I made that choice, a peace flooded my soul and I knew that God was going to take care of me. Not long afterward, I went through a basic twelve-step program, taught by my pastor in Tulsa, and experienced an intense deep healing. Not only was I healed, but my eyes were also opened and I was filled with an understanding of things as never before. I realized that I had certain self-defeating behaviors and that, if I didn't get a grip, I was going to repeat the cycle. I had to take responsibility for Max Davis. I also realized that I was not unique in this. *Everyone* has weaknesses and strengths. It is just as important to know your weaknesses as it is to know your strengths.

It was then that I thought, "God has seen me through so much, and taught me so much. Now I can be a pastor again!" But who would hire a freshly divorced man to pastor his or her church?

Enter Miracle Series #2

I had been writing down all that I had learned, and I began to have a longing in my heart to spread the message of what I had witnessed of God's healing power. One morning at three, I got up because I couldn't sleep and began to pray. And then I knew—I would self-publish this message. I also knew it would cost money to get a venture like this off the ground, and I didn't have any. I prayed and asked God, if this was His will, to help me. I felt God say, "Go in boldness and humility." Fumbling over my words, I humbly went asking investors to help.

As an answer to my prayer, God helped me raise the money I needed! It was a miracle and I was in business.

To our amazement, my self-published book, *Never Stick Your Tongue Out at Mama and Other Life-Transforming Revelations,* started selling out in bookstores. I received phone calls and letters from readers, telling me how the book had changed their lives.

In the midst of all my excitement, I had yet another prophetic dream. This dream was vivid, like the one about Lawrence, Kansas, except this time I was in New York City. I saw the streets, the yellow taxis, and the traffic jams. It made no sense to me, because at that time I knew very little about the publishing industry and did not know that most of the major publishers were located in New York City. The dream had such an impact on me that the next morning I discussed it with my mother-in-law. She responded to me by saying, "I think it has something to do with your book." A few short months later, I was introduced to someone who passed my book on to an agent in New York. That agent helped me find a publisher, part of one of the largest publishing companies in the world. Now I travel to New York a couple of times a year. With my books has come the opportunity to speak to groups around the globe.

What makes this story so remarkable is that twenty-some-odd years ago, God spoke to my heart telling me I was going to be an author and speaker. On the beaches of the Comite River, I envisioned what is unfolding right now. Yet, the fulfillment of this is coming about in a way that I could never have imagined or planned. And it wasn't until I had "died" to my own ego, and myself, and was facing impossible circumstances, that God came through. Losing everything forced me to truly depend on God. Every day I am reminded of the odds of my getting published by a big publisher. I'm just a country boy from Greenwell Springs, Louisiana. Why would they want me? Only God could open the doors He's opened for me.

The most overpowering message in this story is not that I became an author but that all those years when I was crying out to God and it seemed that He wasn't there, He was. He was there when I was a frustrated truck driver. He was there when I was a pastor. He was there during the pain of my divorce. Everything I went through was to get me to this point. God was there all along, teaching me, nurturing me. I've come to a living application of Romans 8:28: *"And we know that in all things God works for the good of those who love him, who have been called according to his purpose."* The word *all* really does mean "all."

Yes, I've researched miracles in other people's lives. Yet I know, personally, that miracles do indeed happen. Give God a chance to work a miracle in your life.

8.

Seven Power Tools for Changing Those Flat Tires in the Rain

Man is a tool-using animal. . . . Without tools, he is nothing.

—THOMAS CARLYLE

My dad can fix anything. I mean it—anything. Over the years, I've come to depend a great deal on his expert ability when it comes to dealing with whatever I have that's broken down. Let's see, he's fixed my washing machine, my refrigerator, my car (a multitude of times), and my air conditioner. You name it; he's fixed it.

As I've grown older, to my surprise, I'm finding that many of my dad's skills have rubbed off on me. But despite my dad's teaching I have the tendency, as a handyman, to delve into a project only to discover halfway through that I don't have the right tools for the job. Let me tell you, there is nothing more frustrating than attempting a relatively simple project and watching it become terribly difficult simply because your tool doesn't fit!

Most of the time it's something really small like a socket that is a millimeter off, or a bolt that is just out of reach. All you need to finish the job is that one little device. So you plunge into your toolbox hoping, wishing, praying that somehow the right thingamajig will be there, but all the while you know perfectly well that you no more have the right tool than a crisp $100,000 bill in your pocket! The search continues, emptying boxes, running to neighbors, or your brother-in-law's, hoping that they will have the golden egg you are looking for. Most of the time, you end up exhausted, outdone, knuckles skinned up, with an unfinished project.

That's me, but it's *not* my dad. This man has tools. He drives a big truck with a big steel toolbox that takes up a third of the space in the truck's bed. I can't tell you how many times he's told me, "Son, no job's that hard if you have the right tools." You'd think I'd get it by now.

What really amazes me is not just that my dad has tools, but he has *power tools!* There is a difference. It's one thing to have the right socket for the right bolt, but when you can have the right tool with power behind it, now that is something to behold.

Once I was helping my dad install an air-conditioning unit. My job was to hang the air vents in all the rooms throughout the house. I had all the right tools—a screwdriver, screws, and a fold-out ladder. But by the time I got to the second room, my arm felt as if it were going to fall off. Dad, noticing my dilemma, pulled out of his toolbox a heavy-duty power drill with a screwdriver bit on the end. What would have taken me an hour, with much pain, now only took a few minutes!

Just as we need physical tools to help us make physical repairs, so we need mental and spiritual tools to help us through the tough life experiences that we sometimes find ourselves in. I would hate to get a flat tire in the rain while driving, only to find out I had no jack or tire-changing kit in the car. When it comes to making the repairs that will get us safely back on the road, we need the right tools, and we need power tools that are plugged into the power source, God.

The following pages contain several power tools to place in your mental and spiritual toolbox. My prayer is that you'll find exactly what your soul needs today!

Tool #1: *Though it may be messy, somtimes you just have to step out into the rain and take control.*

> *If you want to manage your problems successfully, you need to take a chance, take charge, and take control!*
>
> —DR. ROBERT SCHULLER,
> *POWER THOUGHTS*

Try to imagine yourself in this situation: It's raining so hard the water is coming down sideways. It's dark. Your car windshield wipers are on high, but they're not even putting a dent in the thick downpour. You're dressed up in your finest outfit, on the way to an important event, when all of a sudden *POW ... thud ... thump ... bump ... bump ... bump.* It only takes a split second for your mind to conclude "Oh no, blowout!" Cautiously you steer the car to the side of the road and turn on the emergency lights. Meanwhile, the rain continues to pour, with no sign of easing up.

You sit for a moment sulking, murmuring to yourself, "What do I do now? Of all the times to have a flat tire, it happens to me while it's pouring down rain. Just my luck." Refusing to accept what's happened, you continue to sit, wishing that somehow the situation would fix itself. But nothing happens. An angel doesn't appear and change the tire for you. Nor does the tire miraculously fill up with air. Finally, reality sinks in and you realize that to get out of this mess you are going to have to take the bull by the horns, open the car door, and step out into the rain, even though it means getting your nice neat outfit dirty and wet.

We hear a lot these days about the necessity of giving up control. And nine times out of ten, after we peel back the layers of issues that sometimes smother our lives, it is not uncommon to find that at the very bottom lies internal conflict about control. Perhaps we have refused to let go of something or someone in our past that caused us pain, or we're so afraid of what might happen in the future that we try to micromanage every detail of life. There is no doubt that liberation comes when we learn to stop trying to control things, situations, and people in life that we can't control. Nevertheless, there are times during the course of our existence when it is absolutely necessary to roll up our sleeves, grit our teeth, and do what has to be done in order to take charge of certain situations before they control us.

What happened to United Airlines flight 232 in Sioux

City, Iowa, several years ago is a shining example of taking healthy control in a difficult situation. With the plane cruising at an altitude of over fifteen thousand feet, the DC-10's center tail engine abruptly exploded, projecting hot shrapnel throughout the tail section and slicing the plane's hydraulic system in the process. The hydraulic system is a vital link to controlling a plane's flaps, wings, and landing gear.

As the plane filled with smoke and plummeted toward the earth, rather than giving in to almost certain death, the pilots and air traffic controller took control. The copilot rushed toward the back of the plane and rigged up a crude hand-operated cable, making an attempt at moving the flaps and wings by hand. Meanwhile, the captain took directions from the controller via radio and relayed instructions to the copilot. The plane did crash-land on the runway, but afterward experts said that without the heroic activity of these three men, the plane would have landed somewhere in the middle of a cornfield and everyone aboard would have died. "It was a miracle that they could even get that plane down in the state of Iowa, let alone on the runway," said one source. Now, that's control! Because someone on United flight 232 took control, 185 people lived. *Without healthy control, people die, dreams fade, and our mountainous problems crush us.*

The pilots of United flight 232 didn't just allow circumstances to dictate their outcome. They took charge and gained control. This was an extreme situation, but the pilots were able to take action that allowed them to save lives. In our own lives, times when we *should* take control are when *fear and pain* are paralyzing us, preventing us from moving forward with the lives God intends for us.

Taking control doesn't mean playing God. It means working hand in hand with God. In the miracle story of my writing career, God indeed opened the doors, but I had to walk through them. On many occasions, walking through those doors was not easy. Some people thought I was a pie-in-the-sky dreamer. Others simply didn't understand me. It required an enormous amount of faith to move forward through each door that God opened. All I could think about were my past failures and how foolish I would look if I failed again. Yet, to live out what I felt was my destiny in God, I had to take control over my fears and take the necessary steps of faith. And that meant taking charge and taking control.

Tool #2: *We all need help sometimes, maybe someone to just hold an umbrella or call the police.*

> *The race of mankind would perish did they cease to aid each other. We cannot exist without mutual help. All therefore that need aid have a right to ask it from their fellow-men.*
>
> —SIR WALTER SCOTT

So you're standing there in the rain. You have your tire jack and lug wrench. You've decided to take control even if it means getting all wet and wrinkled. But as you get started, you realize that you are not physically able to turn the lug nuts, much less lift the tire off the axle. What do you do? You ask for help. There is no shame in asking for help.

For some reason, we have an ingrained prejudice against asking for help. I know some people who would rather die trying to "fix" a problem by themselves than ask for a little help. Others may realize that they need help but are unable to simply ask for it. To them, asking for help is admitting to weakness or need. But the ability to ask for help without feeling threatened is one sign of personal security.

In the professional sales arena, almost all the top salespeople will tell you that at the end of a sales presentation, simply asking for the sale is one of the hardest things to do. Yet, when salespeople actually ask customers to buy their product, their sales numbers increase significantly. In seminar after seminar, salespeople are trained to remember to ask for the sale. Why? Why do they have to be trained to ask? Because there is a stigma attached to asking for anything. Whether it is asking for a sale or asking for help. But it is okay to ask, because all of us, from time to time, need help.

Some say Jesus Christ was and is the Son of God. Some believe He was a great moral teacher. Others say Jesus lived at a higher consciousness, totally connected with the universe. Almost everyone would agree that Jesus was one of the most influential people in history. Society was forever altered because of Christ. Even time is measured by His birth. Christmas has become the world's most celebrated holiday.

All this because of one man? Think of the power

that must have emanated from Him. If there was ever a person who had his act together, it was Jesus Christ.

Yet, this pillar of world history, this icon in time, needed help. Even He could not fulfill His mission alone. On the way to His crucifixion, Jesus could not even carry His own cross. Because of His battered condition, Jesus was too weak. When He had reached the end of His endurance and was physically broken and wounded, a friend was ordered to pick it up and carry it for Him.[48]

Let me ask you a question. If Jesus Christ, the most together person in the universe, could not carry His own cross, what makes you think you can carry yours? It has been said, "No man is an island." It doesn't mean we are somehow less if we need help and support from others. Pope Leo XIII said, "No one is so rich that he does not need another's help; no one so poor as not to be useful in some way to his fellow man; and the disposition to ask assistance from others with confidence and to grant it with kindness is part of our very nature."

Tool #3: *Stay calm, don't panic; things are rarely as bad as they seem.*

> *Someone once told me that fear is an acronym for the phrase "false evidence appearing real."*
>
> —BARRY FARBER,
>
> *DIAMONDS IN THE ROUGH*

Let's face it. There is never a good time to have a flat tire in the rain. When was the last time you were driving along, wearing your oldest clothing, wrench in hand, with nowhere to go and nothing to do? And when we do have a flat tire in the rain, it usually feels as if our life has come to a halt. In the practical since, it has. Everyone around you is continuing on his or her way, but you are stuck and stranded, unable to get to your destination or fulfill your obligation, until you get that darned tire fixed.

These types of experiences scream for our attention. They force us to stop whatever else we were doing and focus totally on them. But in our minds, we think we can't stop. We have places to go, people to see, bills to pay. We feel that we have to keep moving, but the reality of the situation says we can't move one single inch until we deal with the issue at hand.

Flat tires in the rain are almost always terribly inconvenient and messy, causing our nice neat plans to get wrinkled and dirty. They make us *feel* as if life is coming apart at the edges.

Events like these squeeze our comfort zones, causing us to feel pressure. And when the pressure is on, if we are not careful, reality can easily get blown out of proportion.

To avoid a mental meltdown, it helps when we can step outside of our situations and stay steady and realize that in time this too shall pass. Recently, a friend of mine, just coming out of crisis, said, "Sometimes I feel utterly overwhelmed by so much stuff, like everything is coming at me all at once. All of my problems seem mingled and meshed so tightly together that all I see is this one huge massive ball of problems that's too immense for me to handle. I feel like I'm going to be crushed. But, when I slow down and take time to examine things up close, I realize it is not one massive ball as I perceived, but rather made up of many smaller individual strands of problems. If I deal with each strand separately, my problems don't seem so massive." Good advice.

Mark Twain once quipped, "Life does not consist mainly—or even largely—of facts and happening. It consists mainly of the storm of thoughts that is forever blowing through one's head." When we allow ourselves to be ruled by inflated perceptions, our fears become magnified and we begin to panic. Panicking is not good. *Frantic people do frantic things.* It's important to bring our thoughts captive to reality.

The following are some ways to cope with problems when we feel ourselves beginning to panic:

〜 Get a pen and paper and write them down. Sometimes when we can see our problems on paper, they don't seem so big.

〜 Analyze each problem separately and put it into perspective.

〜 Never make a serious decision when tired, sick, discouraged, or grieving.

When we can see each situation in its proper perspective, we can then investigate the proper way to respond to it and transcend it.

Tool #4: *Don't forget to clean up.*

> *Humanity is never so beautiful as when praying for forgiveness, or else forgiving another.*
> —JEAN PAUL RICHTER

After having and changing a flat tire in the rain, it is important to clean up. You have to wash the grease off your hands, change clothes, and maybe even take a bath. One thing is for sure: You cannot continue on as you are.

When we refuse to let go of bitterness and hold on to unforgiveness from past events in our lives, it is as if we are going through life with greasy hands and soiled clothes, smelling of pessimism. Everything we touch will be affected.

Children amaze me. Not just mine, but children in general. They are incredibly resilient and forgiving. I can't tell you how many parenting mistakes I've made and had to ask for my children's forgiveness. You know, "Daddy was wrong, honey. I'm sorry. Will you forgive me?" Almost always they'll respond by saying something like "Okay, Daddy!" and then jump in my lap to read a book or watch TV as if nothing had ever happened—forgetting, almost instantly, that they had to write fifty lines or were grounded for a week or had to sit in that boring corner for twenty minutes.

Now I'm no parenting expert, but I have learned one principle of successful parenting: Admit your mistakes and say you are sorry. It sounds easy, but trust me, it's not. Many adult children are holding grudges against their parents or are living in dysfunction because their parents never could admit they were wrong and ask their child's forgiveness. And many adult children are living in bitterness because they refuse to forgive their parents.

One day my two daughters and two nieces were spending the day together, and I overheard an unusual ceremony taking place in the hall bathroom. When I listened more closely, I could hardly believe my ears. The four girls were holding hands and had formed a circle. Each one had a separate sheet of paper on which was written all the things she was angry about regarding the others. Each girl took a turn reading her paper out loud. I recall one saying, So-and-so leaves me out. Another one said, We always do what so-and-so wants to do. Another one said, So-and-so hurt my feelings. And around the circle they went. Then they collected all the papers, said a prayer over them, tore them up, and flushed the pieces down the toilet! Immediately, they went outside and proceeded to play as if nothing had ever happened.

Incredible! We need to live like that. We need our systems cleansed of bitterness and unforgivingness, both toward others and ourselves. We also need to let go of grudges we are holding against God.

The key that opens the door to God's best in our lives is forgiveness. Freedom and joy come through the wounds of forgiveness. Holding on to bitterness will sap and drain the flow of blessing from your soul. It will paralyze your effectiveness in life. On top of that, experts are able to trace many physical sicknesses and ailments to holding on to long-term negative emotions. We must have cleansing and release.

With God's help, you can forgive and let go of self-destructive bitterness. Here are some tips:

〜 *Admit* that you are angry and bitter about a particular situation or person.

〜 *Understand* that it is damaging to your well-being.

↬ *Admit* that you, too, make mistakes and are not perfect.

↬ *Stop* talking to others about your bitterness unless it is a counselor or a single trusted friend who will be honest with you.

↬ *Start* talking to God about your bitterness.

↬ *Soak* your soul in the Scriptures and read other material describing how others have overcome similar difficulties.

↬ *Look* forward, not backward.

Tool #5: *Stop under a sheltering tree or overhang.*

> *Facing the possibility of one's own death can cause you to see the richness in life. Of the richest things in life, your friends are the greatest!*
>
> —WOMAN DYING OF CANCER

When it's pouring down rain and a flat tire happens, there is no more precious sight than a large tree or an overhang that you can pull your car under to shield you from a good portion of the rain and make changing the tire much easier.

You know, friends are like that. Shortly before his death, the poet Samuel Taylor Coleridge wrote, "Friends are a sheltering tree." Doesn't that say it all? When life turns on the heat, friends are sheltering trees that provide the cool reassurance we need. In the midst of life's battering storms, friends are sheltering trees that provide us much needed protection from the pounding elements.

My grandmoma impresses me to no end. (I know, it's suppose to be "grandmother," but I call her grandmoma.) She has a plethora of friends, most of them life-long ones. In fact, she has so many friends I sometimes get confused. I'm always calling them uncle or aunt because growing up, I assumed I was related to most of them, but I'm not. They're just good friends—friends who have been so close, for so long, that they've become just like family.

Over the years, Grandmoma and her friends have seen one another through a lot of hard times. Time and time again they have called on one another for support. When Grandmoma gave birth to twins, with six other children to tend to, her friend Norma came over almost daily to help out. Norma would feed and bathe the kids and cook and wash clothes—even clean house and do the dishes. Norma did this until Grandmoma was able to do it for herself.

Good friends are as basic to life and health as water. Ann Kaiser Stearns wrote in *Living Through Personal Crisis,* "The most self-loving action any of us perform in a lifetime is learning how to develop and sustain close friendships. Friends within the family and friends outside the family are the two most essential sources of caring."[49]

Now, I realize that having friends involves risks. Just as we all need friends, so most of us have been either hurt or disappointed in the past by friends and family. Yet, we can't give up. A preacher put it this way. He said, "There were thousands of animals aboard Noah's ark, for a long time, with limited ventilation. Do you know what that meant? There was a whole lot of animal dung. But despite the stench, the ark was the only boat afloat."

Sure, family and friends disappoint us from time to time and even hurt us. But without the comfort and love of other human beings, we will surely sink like lead in the storms of life.

"So, how do I get friends?" you may ask. Simply be one.

Tool #6: *Enjoy the journey. It may make a flat tire in the rain an adventure instead of a pain and your eventual arrival more fulfilling.*

> *A contented man is the one who enjoys the scenery along the detours.*
>
> —GEORGE HERBERT

One of my most cherished memories is of a storm—not a rainstorm, but a snowstorm. I was on a vacation with my father, mother, and sister traveling through the Rocky Mountains when the traffic came to a sudden halt because of a massive blizzard. It was not a life-threatening situation because several miles ahead, highway workers were preparing the road for passage. However, we did sit in the car for several hours, idling away almost a half tank of gas.

As we were waiting, with the car idling, I looked out the window and saw, about two hundred yards in the distance, an old log chapel right at the foot of a mountain. I got out of the car and tromped through the snow to check it out. It was very old and rustic and, surprisingly, unlocked. When I entered, I couldn't believe my eyes. The whole back wall was a huge plate-glass window that overlooked a snow-covered mountain valley. Hanging in the center of the window was a large, rugged, wooden cross. It was one of the most beautiful sights I had ever seen. I sat down in a rugged pew, facing the window, and had an encounter with God. It was awesome. Peace flooded my soul as I was caught up in God's wonderful creation. It's a moment that I would never have experienced, had it not been for the snowstorm. We would have passed the chapel and not even noticed it.

Enjoying the journey is much more important than arriving at the destination because when we take pleasure in the process, not just the result, we are able to soak up life more fully, and we usually live at a more balanced pace. When our lives are more balanced, we can pay more attention to the wonders around us and, most important, to the people around us. When we have this mindset, life's little setbacks and delays become much easier to handle; we enjoy the people God has placed in our lives, and the fulfillment of our life's goals is more rewarding.

Over ten years ago, the San Antonio Spurs basketball team drafted seven feet two David Robinson with hopes that he would lead them to the NBA World Championship. But year after year, the Spurs would play well during the season only to come up short and lose in the playoffs. It seemed as if they would never win the big one.

But finally, after ten long years, they did. In an interview with Jay Leno, after winning the championship, Robinson was asked what it felt like to win it all. He responded, "Winning the world title was very exciting, but not nearly as much as the ten years getting there." David Robinson understood the value of enjoying the journey.

It is important to have goals and a vision of the big picture in life, but if we are too focused on the future, we miss the now, and the now is the most important time of our lives.

It's impossible to truly enjoy the journey and not see the importance of the now or the people involved in the now. On the other hand, when we are overly focused on the destination, we often miss the now and can overlook the people around us. And the people God has placed in our lives are the most important assets we have. Without them, arriving at our destination has significantly less meaning. Relationships are what make life meaningful—relationships with friends, family, and God.

When the final seconds ticked off the clock at the Alamodome and the Spurs finally won the NBA World Championship, the crowd of 39,514 went wild. Fans rushed onto the court along with cameramen and journalists. Amid all the hoopla, a camera picked up David Robinson hugging his young son.

This was a special moment because, as Robinson later told Jay Leno, during the season, and particularly the NBA playoffs, Robinson had spent a lot of time on the road. This particular game was the final one of a seven-game series against the New York Knicks—provided the Spurs won. A Spurs loss would have meant traveling back to New York to play another game against the Knicks. Robinson had told his son that if the Spurs won, he would be home and the two of them could spend time together. When the crowd rushed onto the court to celebrate the world championship, Robinson's son ran on the court to hug his dad, not because the Spurs had won a championship, but because he was happy his dad was going to get to come home.

That story puts everything in perspective, doesn't it? We tend to place so much emphasis on winning, on getting to the top. But to David Robinson's little boy, success was measured in time spent with his dad. I'm sure you've heard the saying, "I've never seen a person on his deathbed say, 'I wish I'd spent more time at the office.'" When we reach the top of whatever we are attempting to do in life, if we haven't enjoyed the journey and people along the way, then the top will be very empty.

Life is brief; we are here for but a moment and then, like a vapor, we are gone. Enjoy the journey and enjoy those who are traveling with you. If you do, a flat tire in the rain just may turn out to be a blessing.

Tool #7: *It's okay if your spare tire doesn't match.*

> *Should you shield the canyons from the windstorms, you would never see the beauty of their carvings.*
>
> —ELISABETH KÜBLER-ROSS

Genesis tells us, "The Lord formed man of the dust of the ground" (Genesis 2:7). Science has confirmed that the elements that make up you and me are the very same ones that make up dirt. It's true.

Unlike earth, however, we have the breath of life in us. As *living* earthen vessels, we have God's spirit inside us. Imagine a candle inside a clay lamp. Second Corinthians 4:7–9 tells us, *"We have this treasure in earthen vessels, that the excellency of the power may be of God, and not of us. We are troubled on every side, yet not distressed; we are perplexed, but not in despair; persecuted, but not forsaken; cast down, but not destroyed."*

As God's vessels, when we take the blows from life that sometimes leave us shouting "That's not fair!" guess what happens? We are not destroyed, and we are not crushed, but we do get cracked. And that is exactly what God wants to happen. You see, with the candle of God's spirit inside our clay vessel, when we get cracked, His light shines out of us. The more cracks in our vessels, the more of God others may see in us.

When others can see joy, peace, and love in the midst of our pain, then they can truly be inspired by the "hope that is within us." Hurting people are rarely interested in our great exploits or our wonderful talents; they want to know about the hope that they can see in us when we are going through some of the same fires they are.

My grandmoma's kitchen contains dozens of wonderful spices, ground into fine powders. When these spices were still on a stem, or in the ground, or in a shell, the flavor and aroma remained within the spice. It is through brokenness, through cracking, that the aromas were released. Without the brokenness or cracking, the sweet aroma wouldn't be experienced.

A crack in our vessels can readily lead to hopelessness. Yet, it can also lead to healing and opportunity. Brokenness can leave us bitter, bemoaning unwanted circumstances and pitying ourselves. Or we can let our brokenness release the aroma of our inner beauty for our healing and the healing of those around us.

Every day I learn more and more that it is okay to be cracked. I don't always have to be perfect or appear perfect. We hear so much about success today that I think some people feel guilty if they are not always bubbling over with happiness and sitting on the top of the world. When we are cracked, though, we can become more compassionate, more understanding, and more tuned in to the needs of others. And touching others is the secret to lasting happiness in life. Here's a thought: When we show our cracks, when we let God's light shine through them instead of trying to hide them, we are becoming real.

To me, nothing demonstrates the value of being real more profoundly than the wonderful children's story *The Velveteen Rabbit,* by Margery Williams Bianco. In it, two stuffed animals, the Skin Horse and the Velveteen Rabbit, were having a conversation in the nursery one day. The conversation went like this:

"What is REAL?" asked the Rabbit one day, when they were lying side by side near the nursery fender, before Nana came to tidy the room. "Does it mean having things that buzz inside you and a stick-out handle?"

"Real isn't how you are made," said the Skin Horse. "It's a thing that happens to you. When a child loves you for a long, long time, not just to play with, but REALLY loves you, then you become real."

"Does it hurt?" asked the Velveteen Rabbit.

"Sometimes," said the Skin Horse, for he was always truthful. "When you are real you don't mind being hurt."

"Does it happen all at once, like being wound up," he asked. "Or bit by bit."

"It doesn't happen all at once, like being wound up," said the Skin Horse. "You become. It takes a long time. That's why it doesn't happen to people who break easily, or have sharp edges, or who have to be carefully kept. Generally, by the time you are Real, most of your hair has been loved off, and your eyes drop out and you get loose in the joints and very shabby. But these things don't matter at all, because once you are real you can't be ugly, except to people who don't understand."[50]

9.

Moving On

The dark threads were as needful, in the weaver's skillful hand, as the threads of gold and silver, for the pattern which he planned.

—GREEK PROVERB

So much has happened since I first began writing this book. I'm not the same person that I was in the beginning. Each day has brought on new challenges and struggles from which I've grown and learned. For example, a few days ago when I was attending a movie with my family, the audience erupted in laughter at a funny line from one of the actors. As the audience roared, I glanced over at my son, James, who had a look of confusion on his face. He had no clue as to what everyone was laughing at. In an instant, another look flooded his face, a look that is hard to describe. It was an out-of-place look, the realization that he was indeed deaf.

I thought I had all my pain under control. But something as small and trite as James missing a punch line in a movie brought it all back. Overwhelmed by waves of hurt, I fought back tears and the desire to walk out of the movie.

Later that day, I went for a long walk. I offered James up to God. I said, "God, I feel like such an inadequate father, but I make the choice to believe that you love James, even more than I do. Take him, God. He's in your hands." Releasing James to God like this has become a ritual with me.

Shortly after my prayer, I was reminded of how faithful God had been to Helen Keller. As you probably know, Helen Keller was both blind and deaf. Yet, despite these obstacles, in an era when there was virtually zero communication with the deaf and blind, God, in His unique way got through to her. Helen Keller refused to be a victim; her life experience has changed our world. Listen to her words:

Difficulties meet us at every turn. They are the accompaniment of life. They result from combinations of character and individual idiosyncrasies. The surest way to meet them is to assume that we are immortal and that we have a Friend who "slumbers not, nor sleeps," and who watches over us and guides us—if we but trust Him.

With this thought strongly entrenched in our inmost being, we can do almost anything we wish and

need not limit the things we think. We may help our-
selves to all the beauty of the universe that we can hold.
For every hurt there is recompense of tender sympathy.
Out of pain grow the violets of patience and sweetness.
The marvelous richness of human experience would
lose something of rewarding joy if there were no limita-
tions to overcome. The hilltop hour would not be half
so wonderful if there were no dark valley to traverse.[51]

Remember, those words were written by someone who could neither see nor hear. If God could take care of Helen Keller in such a magnificent way, surely He can take care of James and also you and me.

God knows right where you are today. Let Him help you transcend those flat-tires-in-the-rain experiences. When you do, you will begin to step through life's puddles and wade through its floods with amazing power and grace.

Notes

1. Charles R. Swindol, *Hope Again* (Dallas: Word, 1997), p. 12.
2. M. Scott Peck, *The Road Less Traveled* (New York: Simon & Schuster, 1978), p. 15.
3. C. S. Lewis, *A Grief Observed* (New York: Bantam, 1963), p. 4.
4. David Wolpe, *The Healer of Shattered Hearts* (New York: Holt, 1990), p. 66.
5. David S. Ariel, *What Jews Believe* (New York: Schocken Books, 1995), p. 29.
6. Rabbi Stewart Vogel, *The Ten Commandments* (New York: HarperCollins, 1998), p. 319.
7. Marjorie Holmes, *How Can I Find You, God?* (New York: Doubleday, 1975), p. 6.
8. Mother Teresa, *The Joy in Loving* (New York: Viking, 1997), p. 82.
9. Jack Canfield, *Chicken Soup for the Christian Soul* (Deerfield Beach, FL: Health Communications, 1997), p. 202.
10. Job 1:1–3.
11. Job 1:3.

12. Job 16:3; 19:2, 22.

13. Job 33:1–3.

14. Job 42:7.

15. Job 2:13.

16. Job 6:13.

17. Job 1:1, 22.

18. Job 42:8.

19. Ibid.

20. Job 19:4.

21. John 16:33.

22. Roy Hicks, *A Small Book About God* (Sisters, OR: Mult-nomah, 1997), p. 161.

23. Job 16:2.

24. Philip Yancey, *Disappointment with God* (Grand Rapids, MI: Zondervan, 1988), p. 181.

25. Job 10:3.

26. Job 19:25; 13:15, 16.

27. Job 38:4, 26, 27.

28. Job 42:3, 6.

29. Medical Center of Baton Rouge report on stress.

30. Sharon Faelten and David Diamond, *Take Control of Your Life* (Emmaus, PA: Rodale, 1988), p. 89.

31. Charles R. Swindol, *Stress Fractures* (Portland, OR: Mult-nomah, 1990), p. 115.

32. Willard Gaylin, *Feelings: Our Vital Signs* (New York: Harper & Row, 1979), p. 52.

33. Isaiah 53:6.

34. Mother Teresa, *The Joy in Loving,* p. 260.

35. Hymn, *It Is Well with My Soul,* by Horatio Spafford.

36. Elaine St. James, *Living the Simple Life* (New York: Hyper-ion, 1996), p. 221.

37. Luke 8:5–15.

38. Julio Melara, "The Truth About Success," audiotape.

39. Luke 18:18–23.

40. Philippians 4:12.

41. Alan Loy McGinnis, *Bringing Out the Best in People* (Minneapolis: Augsburg, 1985), p. 176.

42. Joyce Meyer, *Managing Your Emotions* (Tulsa: Harrison House, 1997), p. 145.

43. Carrie Boyko, *Hold Fast Your Dreams* (New York: Scholastic, 1996), pp. 129–30.

44. Paul Yonggi Cho, *The Leap of Faith* (Gainsville, FL: Bridge-Logos Publishers, 1984), pp. 40–44.

45. Melvin Morse, *Transformed by the Light* (New York: Villard, 1992), p. 102. Reprinted by permission of Villard Books, a division of Random House, Inc.

46. You can read the entire fascinating story in Herb's book *Fighting Cancer with Christ* (Carol Stream, IL: Creation House). The book can be ordered from Mjorud Evangelistic Assoc., 3604 Coolidge N.E., Minneapolis, MN 55418.

47. Ken Gaub, *God's Got Your Number* (Green Forest, AR: New Leaf Press, 1998).

48. Matthew 27:32.

49. Ann Kaiser Stearns, *Living Through Personal Crisis* (New York: Ballantine Books, 1984), p. 69.

50. Margery Williams Bianco, *The Velveteen Rabbit* (New York: Doubleday).

51. Helen Keller, *My Religion* (copyright 1927). Quote taken from *Dale Carnegie's Scrap Book* (copyright 1959 by Dale Carnegie & Associates).

About the Author

Max Davis received an undergraduate degree in journalism from the University of Mississippi, and a master's degree in theology/counseling from the American Bible College and Seminary. He also has done divinity work at Oral Roberts University. Davis has served as pastor and counselor and now devotes his time to writing and public speaking. He lives with his family outside Baton Rouge, Louisiana.

For speaking information, write:

Max Davis
22083 Greenwell Springs Road
Greenwell Springs, LA 70739

Or email: max@iol27.com